Relentless Faith for Uncertain Times

Funmbi Ariyo

TRILOGY CHRISTIAN PUBLISHERS
Tustin, CA

Trilogy Christian Publishers
A Wholly Owned Subsidiary of Trinity Broadcasting Network
2442 Michelle Drive
Tustin, CA 92780

Relentless Faith for Uncertain Times

Copyright © 2024 by Funmbi Ariyo

Scripture quotations marked NKJV are taken from the New King James Version®. Copyright © 1982 by Thomas Nelson. Used by permission. All rights reserved.

Scripture quotations marked AMP are taken from the Amplified® Bible (AMP), Copyright © 2015 by The Lockman Foundation. Used by permission. www.Lockman.org.

No part of this book may be reproduced, stored in a retrieval system, or transmitted by any means without written permission from the author. All rights reserved. Printed in the USA.

Rights Department, 2442 Michelle Drive, Tustin, CA 92780.

Trilogy Christian Publishing/TBN and colophon are trademarks of Trinity Broadcasting Network.

Cover design by Jeff Summers

For information about special discounts for bulk purchases, please contact Trilogy Christian Publishing.

Trilogy Disclaimer: The views and content expressed in this book are those of the author and may not necessarily reflect the views and doctrine of Trilogy Christian Publishing or the Trinity Broadcasting Network.

10 9 8 7 6 5 4 3 2 1

Library of Congress Cataloging-in-Publication Data is available.

ISBN: 978-1-68556-883-2

E-ISBN: 978-1-68556-884-9 (ebook)

Contents

Dedication v

Introduction vii

Chapter One. Intimidation War 1

Chapter Two. My Picture Frame 32

Chapter Three. Roadblocks 53

Chapter Four. Shadow Fighting 68

Chapter Five. Big Bully 87

Chapter Six. Failure Hero 102

Chapter Seven. No One Wins 121

Chapter Eight. Confusion Cloud 136

Chapter Nine. Distractions, Distractions, Distractions... 157

Chapter Ten. Restoration Fire 175

The Prayer of Salvation 198

Dedication

I dedicate this book to those taking their stand in faith and refusing to move and concede the ground they have taken. Without faith, it is impossible to please God. Surrounding us is a great cloud of witnesses who have their own stories of victory in faith. This hour is not the time for us to draw back in unbelief but to continue looking on to Jesus—the Author and Finisher of our Faith.

Firstly, I want to thank God for blessing me with the grace to write so I can be a blessing to others.

I also thank my senior pastors: Pastor Sola Fola-Alade and Pastor Bimbo Fola-Alade. Thank you for everything you have invested in my faith walk.

Finally, I extend my arms of faith and love to my family, who are my most incredible supporters. Thank you for your endurance, even when seemingly nothing was there on the horizon.

Introduction

During my dramatic personal transformation journey amidst the global pandemic, I conceived this book. It showcases the many wars raging around the faith of a Christian believer, which I experienced from intimidation, fear, wrong focus, distractions, and much more. In the book, I share spiritual insights revealed as I leaned into my relationship with God in dealing with these attacks. The knowledge in this book will help ignite overcoming faith in the reader's heart as the book has many practical biblical and life examples.

During the global pandemic, the apple cart of what we held dear was truly upset for many Christians. This book provides a timely reminder that faith exists for challenging and difficult circumstances. It is an essential part of every believer's spiritual DNA.

All we need is the word of the Master spoken to us to step out in confidence despite unsettling circumstances all around. We must leave behind our comfort as we seize a unique opportunity to exercise our faith relentlessly in these troubling times. The world watches in disbelief and witnesses in amazement the miracle of the Christian faith.

I also wrote this book for spiritually hungry believers who want to experience the power of God—believers who are curious about exploring and having their unique adventures of faith and those determined to live in the everyday victory that faith brings. Enjoy the read!

Chapter One

Intimidation War

Faith is such an important subject because when it is activated, it can bring the fullness of God's power into Christian living. Without faith, a believer can limit God's power in their lives, which is far from pleasing for Him (Hebrews 11:6). Faith to a believer is what fuel is to a car. Without it, there is no movement.

As we scroll through *the Book of Hebrews*, we collide with one of the fathers of faith—Abraham.

Called by God, Abraham showed a clear example of enduring faith through his life. He stepped out in obedience, not knowing where he was going but desperately trusting God regardless (Hebrews 11:8).

Abraham not only trusted God to appear, he also trusted Him enough to wait. Abraham patiently waited for God to build a city that would be inherited by those who came many generations after (Hebrews 11:9). Abraham needed to stretch the curtain of his mind, counteracting his natural emotions to accept the Lord's invitation to become a visionary (Genesis 15:5–6).

As a visionary, Abraham took a once-in-a-lifetime opportunity to stare through the eyes of faith. He would see what God told him would be his inheritance one day, though nothing was physically there on the horizon (Genesis 13:14–15). Following his vision, he endured many long years of repeated humdrum, waiting and waiting.

In Abraham, we see a gritty glimpse of the real-life sacrifices and adjustments needed to remain obedient. The same life-changing choices of obedience and flexible adjustments are equally open to believers today.

Littering my life story are many examples of my sacrifices through suffering disappointments, demotions, ridicule, and rejections. Like Jesus, I learned obedience through the things I suffered (Hebrews 5:8).

CHAPTER ONE   INTIMIDATION WAR

I was intimidated by fear and unbelief directly aimed at making me crawl past God's promises and back into retreat and isolation. I had to fight their intimidating grip by speaking the word of faith over those same promises. My confidence was boosted by an unshakable trust in God's restorative power, even when circumstances were saying otherwise.

Abraham's decisions would have a generational impact because God did not just make the promises to him alone but to generations after him. Similarly, I knew this battle was not just about me but about generations who would either succeed or fail based on my decisions. The victory of faith always holds for many generations. My prayer is that generations after me will thank me for the sacrifices I made today.

Sometimes priceless keys to understanding are provided when one asks the right questions (Luke 2:46). This chapter is all about my generational fight against intimidation. To help us further explore the context of this fight, we will consider three critical questions from three books in the Bible. These will be the books of Ephesians, 1 Timothy, and 2 Timothy, as we hit the ground running from the outset of our faith adventure.

In the middle of the sixth chapter of *the Book of Ephesians*, we see a clear outline of the armor of God. The book describes each part of the armor and its purpose. It tells us to put on the whole armor of God. We look at the first of our three questions to gain a deeper understanding of the purpose of the armor. Why would we need armor if we are not in a war (Ephesians 6:10–20)?

Moving on from Ephesians, let's look at our second question: why does Paul warn Timothy to wage warfare described as good concerning the prophecies spoken over him (1 Timothy 1:18)?

Finally, our third question: why does Paul also tell Timothy not to be entangled with the things of this life but to be a good soldier of Jesus Christ who has called him (2 Timothy 2:4)?

These three questions suggest an embroiling and ongoing war.

Let's hold on to our thoughts on the armor for now. We will return to it shortly. Before then, we must take a life-changing detour to talk about salvation. So hold on, dear readers, there may be somebody who needs to take a detour on this journey with us.

Salvation

Second Corinthians 4:4 says the God of this world has blinded people lest they should see the light of the glorious gospel.

> *whose minds the God of this age has blinded, who do not believe, lest the light of the gospel of the glory of Christ, who is the image of God, should shine on them.*
>
> 2 Corinthians 4:4 (NKJV)

I will tell a story that should resonate with many reading this book. It is a story of a young woman who spent many years groping in darkness. She was addicted to finding love in the wrong places, trying to heal a wound of unworthiness that plagued her early life. She masked this sense of unworthiness with ambition and independence. Her achievements were a badge of affirmation that provided concealment from the hurts of the past.

This young woman encountered the gospel of Jesus Christ at a worship concert. Suddenly, light dawned on her as she recognized her life so far had been lived in deep, deep darkness. She heard truths that set her free from the condemnation of a sinful life lived far away from the original plan of Christ for her.

A deep conviction overwhelmed this fragile young woman as she took the tentative steps to accept Jesus as her Lord and Savior. New love and joy flooded her life, and she felt an indescribable peace for the first time in her life.

Now many of us can connect with this young woman's story because, at the heart of her story, we recognize it as a thread in our own life stories. Some are experiencing that story even as they read this book—our detour was for you.

Salvation is the first significant milestone for any believer of Jesus Christ. The landmark of salvation is a translation from one kingdom characterized by darkness, lies, fear, and condemnation to another realm characterized by light, truth, love, peace, and acceptance.

CHAPTER ONE   INTIMIDATION WAR

Every one of us needs love and acceptance.

Many are living "in the dark" right now without the knowledge of the gospel of Jesus Christ. They are like that young woman until they hear the gospel preached, and then light dawns in their darkness (Matthew 4:16).

What does it mean to be living in the dark? Imagine entering a dark room. What is our first instinct? Most likely to turn on the light. In many corners of the world, people do not have the privilege of turning on a physical light. When day turns to night in those areas, they live in physical darkness.

That is a sad and distressing notion; many of us should take a much-needed pause to consider our privilege, which we often take for granted. However, an even more alarming situation relates to those living in spiritual darkness. They are living with a desperate need for the lights to turn on in their lives. The gospel preached to them about enlightenment to come.

As I said before, this life-changing detour was for somebody reading this book. This detour will provide you with an early opportunity, if you want to take it up, to go straight to the chapter on salvation at the end of this book to turn on the lights. Once there, you can make a choice to read through it and take that bold step of commitment from the outset of this book, like the fragile but brave young woman we just encountered. Rest assured, you will also get other opportunities to do so as we progress through this book.

After our needed short detour, as promised, we return to our opening thoughts on the armor of God. One of the parts of the armor listed in Ephesians 6:10–20 is the helmet of salvation. We use this to answer our original opening question: why would we need armor if we were not in a war?

Most believers will recognize that we are indeed in a battle of sorts, hence the strong military symbology used by Paul in the Book of Ephesians. However, this is not a physical war but a spiritual war waged on the battleground of our lives. In this spiritual war, the vital helmet of salvation covers our heads where our precious mind rests, safe from any attacks.

Darkness in our minds kept many of us from taking that first step in our salvation journey early on in our lives. The darkness generally centered on what we knew about God and equally what we knew about ourselves. We had to tackle this darkness to enter God's kingdom of light through the acceptance of Jesus Christ as our Savior.

There is a common saying that in areas where we lack knowledge, we are "in the dark." The expression presents darkness as a lack of knowledge. Light, in startling contrast, however, represents an abundance of knowledge.

Armed with some more knowledge of God and His love for us, many have decided to accept Jesus, God's Son, as their Savior.

Our acceptance rested on a once and for all eternity battle for victory for us. Jesus Christ settled that on the Cross (John 19:17–42, John 20).

The same signed and sealed victory now precedes our ongoing daily Christian battle to maintain that victory experience in our lives.

In this daily battle, the armor and the helmet of salvation ensure we continually maintain our victory after salvation. That essential helmet provides a reminder that we must always flood our minds with the light of what salvation means to us throughout our Christian journey.

By doing this, we are putting on our helmet of salvation.

We have all experienced the daily stresses of this once-in-a-lifetime global COVID pandemic. What we experienced has helped us appreciate the mind's fragility.

We have discovered that the mind requires a conscious focus and attention on the right things. The proper attention brings much-needed light to help the mind remain healthy and in the excellent condition God originally intended. The things we took for granted in the mind's hidden nature before the pandemic can no longer be overlooked, even in the believer's life.

Now that we have covered salvation and related it to the first element of the armor of God, *the helmet of salvation*, we move on in our faith adventure.

CHAPTER ONE   INTIMIDATION WAR

Fear

A lot of bullying has to do with intimidation and fear. Children and adults who have endured any type of bullying at some point in their lives understand that.

As well as physical bullying, we can also endure spiritual bullying.

Second Timothy 1:7 (NKJV) says the following:

For God has not given us a spirit of fear, but of power and of love and of a sound mind.

This scripture opens our eyes to the reality that fear is a spirit. With that understanding, we see that spiritual bullying is possible. The spirit of fear can be a bully. It can intimidate us if we allow it. How do we counteract its intimidation? We go to its roots. Let us look to the farmer for help.

In bygone years, farmers used a sharp ax to tackle the roots when they had a problem with weeds.

Similarly, to tackle spiritual weeds like fear, we also need the sharp spiritual ax of God's Word to tackle the problem's origins. If we can deal with the roots, we can solve the problem.

However, it is not just enough to tackle the problem. That is just the first step. You can get rid of all the weeds and be no closer to the harvest as a farmer. The weed clearing is just preparing the ground to plant something. It will be foolhardy to declare victory just by clearing the land. We must take the next step to plant a good seed for the harvest. The real success comes from the harvest, especially an abundant one.

Now, let us press in for our abundant spiritual harvest as we observe a different spirit from fear in this same scripture. This spirit resides at the opposite end of the spectrum from fear—one characterized by power, love, and a sound mind. I present to you the Holy Spirit. That is the greatest gift the Lord Jesus gave to all believers in Him.

We see the Holy Spirit described as our Helper in the scripture below. An expanded version of the word Helper means **C**omforter, **H**elper, **A**dvocate, **S**trengthener, **I**ntercessor, **S**tandby. Adding an extra **S** shows the Holy

Spirit is indeed my **CHASSIS**, which means the car of my life is not moving anywhere without Him!

> *"If you love Me, keep My commandments.*
> *"And I will pray the Father, and He will give you another Helper, that He may abide with you forever—*
> *"the Spirit of truth, whom the world cannot receive, because it neither sees Him nor knows Him; but you know Him, for He dwells with you and will be in you.*
> *"I will not leave you orphans; I will come to you."*
> John 14:15–18 (NKJV)

Dwelling With and In You

The closer we get to the spirit of love, power, and a sound mind, the further we get from the spirit of fear. The two cannot coexist. To abide and dwell in one is to depart from the other.

A runner knows that the further they get away from the starting block, the closer they get to the finish line.

We must be like that runner putting a clear distance between us and the spirit of fear. We must get as far away from it as possible by determining to get closer to the Holy Spirit, the CHASSIS of our lives.

We may also need to ask ourselves some honest questions about where we live today. Are we living in "fearville" or "victoryville"? From my experience, fear generally brings paralysis to our spiritual walk, so we are like hamstrung horses who have become lame. Fear aims to paralyze our movement in faith. When fear has the upper hand, I find myself rooted to one spot where previously I had momentum and rapid movement towards a goal or assignment.

If we look at the *David and Goliath* story in the Bible, we can see that it also highlights even more clearly that faith and fear cannot coexist. One must defeat the other. God fuels one, and the enemy and lies fuel the other.

What defeated Goliath? I present to you the single stone which brought an outsize problem down to the ground of defeat: the Word of God.

Only one stone, strategically used, was all David needed. A faith-filled boy who knew what his God could do rose beyond the prevailing atmosphere of fear. He propelled the prepared stone into the direction of a

CHAPTER ONE   INTIMIDATION WAR

massive problem taunting a nation, promptly shattering the enemy's lies and taunts in defeat. He refused to believe the report that said he could not triumph over Goliath.

In the Old Testament, stones represented covenant and eternal things. The pillar of stone, like the one Jacob set up, was a reference point for a covenant encounter he had with God (Genesis 28:18). Stones also symbolized eternal memorials, as we saw with Joshua as Israel crossed over the Jordan into the promised land (Joshua 4:1–9). There are many Old Testament examples we see further explained in the New Testament in the Bible.

In the Biblical books of Matthew, Mark, and Luke in the New Testament, the stone the builders rejected has now become the cornerstone (Matthew 21:42, Mark 12:10, Luke 20:17). This stone spoke of Christ (Acts 4:11) and the Word Himself becoming flesh (John 1:14).

We must be like David, who was unwilling to entertain fear in his life. We must not dwell in the spirit of fear but in the spirit of love, power, and a sound mind. We must meet fear head-on with the tried and tested stone of the Word, representing Christ.

Out of Christ flows the spirit of love, power, and a sound mind.

Resisting Fear

When most people think of a roaring lion, the image brings fear to many hearts. A roaring lion is not your beloved dog, cat, or fish; that brings a vision of love that warms your heart. We see the enemy portrayed as one who goes about like a roaring lion seeking whom he may devour (1 Peter 5:8).

In the following verse of this scripture, we see that we are to resist the devil, steadfast in the faith (1 Peter 5:9).

Fear is a weapon Satan usually deploys in strategic seasons, sometimes called opportune times (Luke 4:13), so in resisting him, we must also fight fear in these seasons.

In our resistance, our stance is not losing our ground of faith. Many of us have taken a lot of ground by our faith in our personal lives, family life, career, business, or ministry. We must resist fear from taking any of that ground from us.

CHAPTER ONE   INTIMIDATION WAR

Many have spent countless hours praying and interceding for the hard-won ground they have now gained. These numerous hours represent our lives. There has been a sacrifice of your life to expand and advance the kingdom of God in these areas. In that context, there will be an alarm ringing in your heart if somebody were to ask you to knowingly surrender this precious ground you have laid down your life to take.

Knowingly is the keyword here. Generally, the enemy aims for you to surrender this unknowingly, sometimes through subtle thoughts and suggestions in your mind. The defeat in the Garden of Eden came as a little thought and suggestion, which ultimately led to an unforeseen eternal impact (Genesis 3:4–24). If Eve had realized the full extent of what she would end up giving away by entertaining those thoughts, she would have resisted the lure of temptation to do so.

There is a reason why "fear not" is a constant charge in the Bible. Fear's yoke is always burdensome and can affect all areas of our lives if left unchecked. When it is left unchecked, fear can ultimately take over and rule our lives. Suddenly, unintended consequences of anxiety and worry come sliding into those who permit fear to have ground in their lives.

It is time for us to repent for allowing fear to have the upper hand in any area of our lives. It is time to admonish ourselves for spending more time listening to the fear reports in many forms of media than listening to the Word, which cultivates faith in our hearts.

Isolation

A community of other believers provides an all-important safety net for all believers. The roaring lion seeking whom he may devour, which we saw in 1 Peter 5:8, is generally looking for the isolated and vulnerable. They represent easy prey he can quickly attack.

Isolation can occur in multiple dimensions. The first dimension is physical, where you become distanced from other believers through offense or unforgiveness. I might as well announce this to many young Christians who may be reading this book. There is no such thing as a perfect church. This idealistic mindset has robbed many believers of the ground they should have gained in their local church.

CHAPTER ONE INTIMIDATION WAR

In the same way, there is no perfect family. There is no ideal church. If we could stick it out, we would find intense beauty in an excellent Christ, perfecting an imperfect family or church through His love. The perfecting nature of Christ gently rubs against our imperfections through His Word and the Holy Spirit as we start to look more like Him.

However, our imperfections are not tackled all at once. Each area represents a mini project to be tackled in love. So we may be a saint in one area of our lives but a terror in another place. That is the beauty of life and relationships. We are fragile beings and generally can handle only so much chastening at any one time. The motive of chastening is love, not destruction (Hebrews 12:5–6), so it is usually heaped to us in small teaspoons at a time, not all at once. God gives us grace for the area of weakness He is addressing now (2 Corinthians 12:9).

Now may be the perfect time to put this book down. The perfecting nature of Christ is all food for thought and probably gives us an excellent opportunity to pause. We may need to revisit some broken relationships as we need to mend them because our understanding was short-sighted in that area until now. All adventures require challenges, so please accept this as a humble challenge before continuing.

Now, we have moved that out of the way. In the same way Jesus taught us (Matthew 5:23–24), let's now continue after reconciliation on our path of discussion about the importance of physical fellowship in fighting isolation.

Suppose we look at the great Apostles in *the Book of Acts*. Even with their immense level of spiritual responsibility, they still walked in teams of two or more. Even they were not above physical fellowship and companionship despite the litany of miracles, signs, and wonders that Jesus granted through them (Acts 14:3).

The other dimension of isolation is spiritual, an attempt to dislocate you from corporate spiritual activities like corporate prayer and corporate worship, which help keep you spiritually connected.

Someone once shared a profound dream they had with me relating to someone who everyone thought was spiritually strong. In the dream, this person, who everybody considered spiritually strong, was hit by a train. Still, others in the dream could not see this, and the person who had the dream could see the incident, so they shouted to others, "Can you not see they are bleeding?"

I believe this dream represented what was going on spiritually with the person hit by the train; they were losing their life spiritually, but others around them could not see it happening. I think the Lord opened the eyes of the person who had this dream to the spiritual reality of what was occurring, which others could not perceive with their natural eyes.

Thank God for the lifesaving protection which came to this person spiritually when this dream was shared and its meaning understood. It came through a spiritual revelation from a dream of a fellow believer. That is the power of our spiritual connection to other believers.

We are not to quench the spirit which forms bonds of spiritual connection between us (1 Thessalonians 5:16–21). It can be a lifesaver for us.

Do not quench the Spirit.
Do not despise prophecies.

Test all things; hold fast what is good.

1 Thessalonians 5:19–21 (NKJV)

With the new insight of understanding we have now gained on the nature of fear, we must also appreciate that not every dream a believer has, is from God. That might be a shock to many readers.

Some dreams have been strategically assigned to believers to bring fear into many lives for a prescribed season. We must always test every dream to determine whether it is from God.

By the grace of the Holy Spirit, this revelation came to me in a season of intense warfare. I knew the heavens were about to break open for me in a particular area of my life. I noticed that my usual pattern of refreshing sleep with Godly dreams had been interrupted, and some unusual dreams emerged. Each of these dreams brought fear into my heart as I encountered various evil-looking animals that intimidated me, and I woke up each time with an overwhelming sense of fear.

We should throw some dreams straight into the spiritual bin. We should not waste any precious time trying to unravel them; they are at best a distraction or, at worst, a dark tunnel to bring us into fear. The Holy Spirit is always there to help us discern what is not from God and what is.

I knew I had to resist fear in this strategic season of my life.

Speaking Faith

The more we know who we are, the more likely we are to speak about ourselves and the less likely we are to be intimidated. If I know, the greater one is in me (1 John 4:4). I cannot be intimidated by any person, circumstance, or challenge.

> *You are of God, little children, and have overcome them, because He who is in you is greater than he who is in the world.*
>
> 1 John 4:4 (NKJV)

Similarly, the more we share the testimony of God's goodness in our lives, the more we are empowered in our faith. It shows the power of our testimony (Revelations 12:11).

> *"And they overcame him by the blood of the Lamb and by the word of their testimony, and they did not love their lives to the death.*
>
> Revelation 12:11 (NKJV)

I recently heard a spectacular testimony of someone being pulled back from the brink of death. The story reverberated through my spirit over twenty-four hours later. In this instance, it was somebody else's shared testimony; imagine the tremendous power held within my testimony for others.

I pray the Lord will give you a new testimony while reading this book. God's Word says He takes us from glory to glory (2 Corinthians 3:18) and faith to faith (Romans 1:17). So, we can also expect to receive fresh new testimonies which demonstrate God's greater glory in our lives as evidence of our growing faith.

We would discover what a great life we had if we constantly played the movie of our lives in our head, watching through the lens of gratitude that continually flows into what we say. As a result, what we experience daily would be far from the draining struggle of a life filled with murmuring and complaining and even further from the feelings of powerlessness and defeat.

I recently went through a period of restoration in which I saw the movie of my life replaying right before my eyes. This time, the Holy Spirit took me on the journey, allowing me to watch this movie through God's lens, not my broken lens.

I grasped the truth about painful past incidents. I was able to see them now through the lens of the God who intervened and intended to deal with the pain but was limited by human actors.

At the end of this movie, I no longer experienced torrents of angry tears and gasps of helplessness. Instead, I felt deep gratitude. The Holy Spirit was helping me to understand the actual script of my life, not the fake copy I had been playing for many years in my mind.

You may want to take some time out to rest and allow God to show you the restored movie of your life. It will now play in your head through His almighty lens.

The movie of our lives is always good because that is what the Word of God tells us. His thoughts and plans for us are always good and not evil. He plans to help us prosper, ultimately giving us hope and a future (Jeremiah 29:11).

The more we see the goodness of God at work in our lives, the more we realize the undeniable nature of God's kindness towards us.

The more we discover the oil of His love, the more we discover that there are still billions of pent-up barrels of His love yet undiscovered (Ephesians 3:17–19).

Restoration Faith

The story of *David and Mephibosheth* is an excellent example of a king's restorative power. In the case of Mephibosheth, the one who held the restoration key was King David. In our case, the restorer is the King of kings. The Greatest Restorer is God.

Like Mephibosheth, many have suffered paralysis in their lives because of a traumatic experience that may have defined them.

That trauma and its crippling nature kept us in the dark in a hidden place like Lo Debar, which was the case with Mephibosheth.

The Great Restorer is here and wants to pour out His restoration power by showing us His love. He will heal us and bring us back to our princely position as joint heirs with Christ.

Like Mephibosheth, our covenant with God through Christ entitles us to that act of restoration. And that restoration covenant is seeking us out now.

> *And the king said, "Is there no longer anyone left of the house (family) of Saul to whom I may show the goodness and graciousness of God?" Ziba replied to the king, "There is still a son of Jonathan, [one] whose feet are crippled."*
>
> 2 Samuel 9:3 (AMP)

The search is on, and the question asked: where is he or where is she, and your name called.

> *So the king said to him, "Where is he?" And Ziba replied to the king, "He is in the house of Machir the son of Ammiel, in Lo-debar."*
>
> 2 Samuel 9:4 (AMP)

You are being brought out of that place of hiddenness and lowliness and into the King's presence.

> *Then King David sent word and had him brought from the house of Machir the son of Ammiel, from Lo-debar.*
>
> 2 Samuel 9:5 (AMP)

However, your covenant is a New Testament covenant higher than the Old Testament one David operated under (Hebrews 8:6). For you, this means your level of restoration will be of the miraculous type of the man who was lame from his mother's womb and received complete physical restoration (Acts 3:2–10). In the Old Testament, David did not have the power to restore Mephibosheth's physical lameness, only his position to sit and eat at the king's table. The name of Jesus Christ, operating by a higher covenant, did both.

Glory to God!

CHAPTER ONE   INTIMIDATION WAR

My Faith Prayer

Lord, help me to overcome every form of intimidation in my life as you show me new dimensions of Your Power.

I can do all things through Christ who strengthens me.
(Philippians 4:13, NKJV)

My Relentless Faith Testimonies

Record here the many ways God has amazed you as you relentlessly stretched your faith.

_____
_____
_____
_____
_____
_____
_____
_____
_____
_____
_____
_____
_____
_____
_____
_____
_____
_____
_____
_____

CHAPTER ONE   INTIMIDATION WAR

Chapter 2

My Picture Frame

We open this chapter by continuing from where we left off in the last chapter with Mephibosheth's story. This chapter is all about identity. We need to recognize that our identity can act as a springboard to how we frame the picture of our lives. When we first meet him, Mephibosheth's identity had taken a severe traumatic knock. When David calls for him in 2 Samuel 9:8 (NKJV), he describes himself as a dead dog.

> *Then he bowed himself, and said, "What is your servant, that you should look upon such a dead dog as I?"*

Never mind that he was a prince through his lineage with King Saul. We can see in the scripture above that Mephibosheth had allowed his circumstances to define him. David did not fall into the same trap of victimhood. Instead of focusing on Mephibosheth's present physical lameness and hiddenness, David focused on the lineage and covenant with his father, Jonathan.

Let's look at another New Testament example. John the Baptist was in the wilderness till the day of his manifestation to Israel (Luke 1:80). The wilderness location did not change his identity or prophecies. When it was time for his emergence, he started preaching the gospel of repentance without any apologies.

We are all guilty of allowing our circumstances to define us. How you see yourself determines your expectations and how others will treat you.

We see this scenario played out also with the spies sent to the land of Canaan, who saw themselves as grasshoppers (Numbers 13:33).

> *"There we saw the giants (the descendants of the Anak came from the giants); and we were like grass-*

hoppers in our own sight, and so we were in their sight."

Numbers 13:33 (NKJV)

We can never rise beyond the level of our identity, which is why this topic is so important. The spies who saw themselves as grasshoppers could never imagine themselves victorious in the promised land.

Their perception of their identity had already defeated them before they stepped into the promised land.

Smallness

How could we see ourselves as small when we serve a big God, and we bear His image and His likeness (Genesis 1:26)?

In the Word of God, we never find ourselves described as small or minor. Yet we often constrain and inhibit what God may be trying to do in our lives through our mindsets.

Those who know their God shall be strong and carry out great exploits, the scripture in Daniel 11:32 reminds us. It does not say we should be weak and defeated—

far from it. Instead, it tells us to expect to see exploits in our lives through our knowledge of God. Can we ask ourselves the question: what great exploits has my knowledge of God produced in my life?

We need to know what has been written concerning us and renew our minds to that perspective (Roman 12:2). Otherwise, our minds can easily conform to our old thinking patterns and behavior based on our life experiences from before our salvation commitment. The Word of God has the power to transform our minds, empowering us to take on new ways of thinking and behavior. Based on the new mirror we are looking into, we can build a new picture frame for our lives (2 Corinthians 3:18).

> *But we all, with unveiled face, beholding as in a mirror the glory of the Lord, are being transformed into the same image from glory to glory, just as by the Spirit of the Lord.*
> 2 Corinthians 3:18 (NKJV)

To have its maximum impact, we must accept the Word of God in its simplicity. We must not argue with it, or even worse still, ignore it and carry on as usual.

In The Parable of the Sower, we see that we would have no problems bearing fruit if we could understand the word (Matthew 13:23). We would obtain conquerors' fruit if we could understand the words about us being more than conquerors.

Yet in all these things we are more than conquerors through Him who loved us.

Romans 8:37 (NKJV)

The more we understand God's Word and what it says about us, the more we can use it to frame our new identity in Christ. In our salvation experience, the old lives we died to have been hidden in Christ so our new life in Christ may become evident (Colossians 3:3).

What lay hidden in God's Word in the Old Testament was revealed by Christ Jesus in the New Testament (Ephesians 3:9).

We are no longer the "dead dog" Mephiphoseth describes himself as in The Old Testament (2 Samuel 9:8), but joint heirs with Christ as the New Testament tells us we are (Romans 8:17).

Warring With Our Prophecies

Some have had some mighty prophecies spoken over them. Some of those prophecies were by God-inspired parents who gave them at our births through the names we carry. Some came from spiritual authority placed over our lives in a way similar to Paul's relationship with Timothy.

We see this beautiful gem illustrated in 1 Timothy 1:18–19.

> *This charge I commit to you, son Timothy, according to the prophecies previously made concerning you, that by them you may wage the good warfare, having faith and a good conscience, which some having rejected, concerning the faith have suffered shipwreck,*
>
> 1 Timothy 1:18–19 (NKJV)

The warfare of faith in Timothy's life was to walk in the fullness of the prophecies concerning him and his spiritual identity. The term used above was good warfare. From this illuminating scripture, we see that it is not enough to receive prophecies about your spiritual identity, which, in essence, is the seed of your spiritual destiny.

Still, the individual who has received the prophecies must also wage good warfare to actualize these prophecies. Otherwise, the thief who comes to steal, kill, and destroy stands on hand to capture any dormant prophecies where the individual has not yet laid a claim on it (John 10:10). This thief, similar to the birds in *The Parable of the Sower* (Matthew 13:3–23), comes to snatch away things sown in our hearts.

Those prophecies released to us usually came after many hours of labor spiritually. We cannot stand idly by while our spiritual heritage is stolen. We must wage a good warfare to secure what is ours and see it fully manifest on earth. There is no usefulness in a prophecy released from heaven to the earth to benefit an individual, then returning to heaven unfulfilled. No, it must hit the mark. It must come to pass just as declared.

Only one person can emerge as the victor when warring with prophecy. Much heavenly blessing is available to you in your war for actualization (Ephesians 1:3). I see you emerging victorious with every God-inspired prophecy spoken over your life. Amen.

I pray you will translate every spiritual blessing which is part of your heritage into reality on earth. Amen.

Warring From a Seat of Victory

We also sometimes do not realize that we are fighting a staged war.

The war is not really for apprehension but for establishment. Let us illustrate this with a story. Imagine you are part of a king's government sent into a land already seized from enemy forces riddled with corruption. Your remit is not to fight the war again for territory. Instead, you are to establish a new pattern for the land, which has now emerged free from the bondage of corruption.

As part of this new pattern, you will also be establishing a new culture in the land, articulating how the land will operate to benefit those living there. The benefits would include a new culture and new working methods predicated not on corruption but on love. Through the help of a powerful supernatural agency of love given by the king, this new government will use every opportunity for all inhabitants to see this love in action.

The story above should be our story as Christians. Jesus Christ already fought the war for apprehension (Colossians 2:13–15). Our following remit is to introduce the culture of love through the message of salvation, presenting the world's inhabitants with the opportunity for a once-in-a-lifetime light for darkness exchange. People will then experience freedom from the bondage of corruption.

We are to act as disciples to the nations by teaching them to observe the new personal laws of the government of Christ. At the same time, we showcase the benefits those laws have had in our own lives and will also have in theirs (Matthew 28:19–20). All elements of our assignment shall be secured through the help of the powerful supernatural love agency of the Holy Spirit.

When we start to do this, we begin to represent the values as ambassadors of a new upside-down kingdom different from the world.

A kingdom realm where those who are foolish, weak, and insignificant become mighty because the glory from all their exploits belongs to their King—Christ (1 Corinthians 1:26–30). Their foolishness, weakness, and insignificance reinforce the reality that any power does not emanate from them. Instead, their lives signpost everything they achieve back to their actual source of glory.

In this new love kingdom, we learn that uneducated and untrained men with no letters behind their names can become powerhouses and restorers (Acts 3). Service can be a gateway to greatness (Acts 6–Acts 8). Murderers can experience conversion by a newly available grace and become ambassadors of this new kingdom's government (Acts 9:1–31). Widows can become heroes (Acts 9:36–43).

A new love kingdom where those who are unqualified on paper qualify by their actions (Acts 10). Persecution can lead to more incredible advances (Acts 8, Acts 12). The supernatural agency of the Holy Spirit can start a new wineskin movement, extending the borders of this government and allowing the flow of this precious new wine to the ends of the earth (Acts 13–Acts 28).

We all love a good story with a good ending. I found the most powerful transformation stories I have ever experienced in the pages of the Bible, *the Book of Life*. However, as we read it, we must never forget that we are warring from a position of victory already secured!

Whose Are You?

To whom do you belong? Each of us has faith, even if it is in Agnosticism that denies God. We either have a singular faith towards God or a plural faith towards many other deities and things.

Your works will reveal whether you belong to God, who is simply defined by love.

The fire in the crucible of life will sooner or later reveal the foundation of our lives, as the materials with which we built our lives, including our works, will be tested (1 Corinthians 3:11–15). Only the solid materials of divine and eternal things can survive the test, with everything else more likely to be burned in the fire.

CHAPTER 2   MY PICTURE FRAME

As we progress in this chapter on identity, know that we cannot talk about the Christian faith without talking again about love. The only fuel for the Christian faith is love. If you do not see results by your faith, then this is the first area where you should run a diagnostic test.

Many owners take their cars into garages and speak to experienced mechanics. These simple conversations can hint at what diagnostics the mechanics will need to run on the car.

Equally, we are designed to run on love. Any other fuel in our tanks starts to cause major havoc in our Christian life. Unforgiveness has corroded many an engine and led to faith failure. Lack of partnership with the oil of the Holy Spirit has led to many a life experiencing the knocking noises of relationship frictions. Subsequently, these frictions cause overheating, with anger and frustration spiralling out of control.

You Will Have What You Say

What we say about ourselves has significant ramifications. We will generally find it challenging to rise beyond what we say about ourselves. Depending on their content, our words can effectively place a welcome, invisible, and immovable open door, or they can close the door on what we can achieve.

Early on in this chapter, I made the statement, "We can never rise beyond the level of our identity," which is why the topic of our words is so important.

Our voice, in essence, expresses through words what we have already internalized about our identity. What we say then becomes an overflowing expression of what we have already internalized.

We see this clearly illustrated in the *Book of Numbers* as we journey with Israel on the cusp of their entry into the promised land, where an open door awaited them. Still, even though the doors were open, the Israelites encountered adversaries. Paul's experience at Ephesus also featured open doors with corresponding adversaries (1 Corinthians 16:9). The two generally go hand in hand.

Faith does not ignore the adversaries. Faith, however, triumphs by believing in a God more powerful than those adversaries. Does your God eat up giants for breakfast? Mine does. Joshua and Caleb understood this, so Caleb said, "Let us go up immediately" (Numbers 13:30). There is always an immediacy to faith. Faith is always now (Hebrews 11:1).

The faith-charged words of one filled with confidence in God always sound unfathomable to those sheltering in doubt.

Their words can sound preposterous, almost like they are determined to ignore the facts. Nevertheless, the one filled with faith is living the reality of the words God has spoken to them through His Word. That has now become their everyday reality—not the natural circumstances that they see.

I have often been awoken from sleep with the Holy Spirit whispering faith-filled words into my ears. The interesting thing is, whenever I obey those words and put them into action immediately, I generally see the results immediately—sometimes within twenty-four hours.

When you look in the mirror, who do you see? A failure or a person reigning victorious in life with Christ (Romans 5:17)?

I have had some breathtaking experiences in which God told me things that seemed impossible. I will share one of them. I remember once, as I was about to go on a trip, God told me He would upgrade me on this trip.

When I arrived at the airport that cold morning and faced the reality of a stone-faced, unsmiling man at the check-in desk, the thought rolled into my mind: how will this happen? "Passport, please; how many pieces of luggage are you checking in?" I continued the conversation, looking for clues and signs that could signal the expected upgrade. There was none, just the churn of logistics.

At the end of the conversation, with my boarding pass handed over, I sighed and glanced at it. I noticed the number of my seat seemed to have changed from what I had selected online a few days beforehand. Immediately, the thought of complaining came to my mind. I did not want a new allocation at the back of the airplane, next to the toilets. However, humility kicked in; I surrendered to whatever God had planned. I was not going to complain.

CHAPTER 2   MY PICTURE FRAME

The next thing I heard jolted me out of my thoughts. The man at the check-in desk was speaking to me, but I could not quite grasp the words I was hearing. "When you go through, go straight to the lounge." My initial reaction was: "Why is he telling me about the lounge?" Then I looked at my boarding pass as I headed past the check-in desk and saw the words that changed my mood. It shifted my countenance from one of resigned indifference to pure joy as the full realization of my upgrade hit me.

I eagerly skipped through the immigration and luggage scan to get to the lounge. I envisioned myself once there, setting my bags down and punching my fist in the air, shouting, "Jesus did it, oh yes, He did!" while the heavy chords chimed on the organ melody playing in my heart.

However, when I got to the lounge, I realized I was in the rarefied air of the business class lounge, and hushed tones surrounded me. So, I did the next best thing and called my sister. I shouted into the phone, "Can you believe they upgraded me?"

We laughed excitedly together as I genuinely rejoiced in what God had done and recounted my whole experience. I heard gasps of "Wow!" at the other end. I even heard the disgruntled voice of my brother-in-law in the background as he complained that he had never received an upgrade during all his travels.

I laughed even harder at the favor of it all. God always does things in style. What do you think happened with my return leg? I was upgraded again, of course. Hopefully, you are now fully connected to the script of this story, which the Great Director in heaven had already orchestrated.

To others, the experience I shared above may seem inconsequential in the grand scheme of life. However, it was a clear affirmation of God's faithfulness to His words at the time for me. God still honored His words to me and brought pure joy into my heart. That is the main essence I wanted to draw out from my story, even in this little example.

Incredible mastery of faith comes from practicing faith, even in the little things. Each time I look into

God's Word and put into action what He says about me, my confidence in God's picture of my destiny increases.

As my confidence increases, my faith grows. A growing faith increasingly ignites the explosive substance of God's Word, so I start to see more outstanding and miraculous results in my life. When I continue to cooperate in faith by playing my part in the script of the future God has already written about me, I please God (Hebrews 11:6).

My Faith Prayer

Lord, help me to have faith to see myself as You see me, so my past does not limit me.

For I know the thoughts that I think toward you, says the LORD, thoughts of peace and not of evil, to give you a future and a hope.
(Jeremiah 29:11, NKJV)

CHAPTER 2   MY PICTURE FRAME

My Relentless Faith Testimonies

Record here the many ways God has amazed you as you relentlessly stretched your faith.

_____
_____
_____
_____
_____
_____
_____
_____
_____
_____
_____
_____
_____
_____
_____
_____
_____
_____
_____
_____

Chapter Three

Roadblocks

We open the curtain on this chapter with an apparent tussle playing out between Moses and Pharaoh. We see this unravel with intrigue in the *Book of Exodus*. It starts in Exodus 5 and goes on until God calls time on this tug of war in Exodus 14.

Freedom means total freedom, which is what Moses was to deliver. However, Pharaoh wanted to drag out a staged negotiation for freedom in one area but not the other. It seemed unimaginable to Pharaoh to let the children of Israel go completely free, totally unchecked. There was always a lurking intent to ensure they lived with one type of limitation or the other.

Place of Sacrifice

The first limitation Pharaoh tried to impose on the children of Israel was on the place for their sacrifice.

Pharaoh offered them an alternative to Horeb, the mountain prescribed by God for their sacrifice, which was a three-day journey in the wilderness. Pharaoh essentially said, stay in this land and offer your sacrifices (Exodus 8:25). He gave them what seemed like a practical and convenient option to the more grueling three-day journey through the wilderness.

However, convenience never outweighs the covenant of obedience. When God prescribes our place of sacrifice, we must obey fully. God determines the location for our sacrifice, not convenience.

Any form of compromise based on convenience would have left the spiritual bondage of disobedience hanging over the Israelites' lives.

It is the same today. Many have settled in churches purely on practical considerations of proximity and hearing a lovely sermon on a Sunday. These situations are more about convenience and not upsetting the tranquillity of our lives than necessarily what God prescribed.

I would suggest you flip through the pages of the Gospels in the Bible. Jesus' messages were anything but a sedate Sunday sermon. They were fiery and challenging. As a result, His messages were very compelling. They placed the mirror of the Word where God intended it—directly in front of us. He did this so we could look in that mirror and see ourselves as we are instead of the airbrushed versions on our social media pages.

Suppose that today you are sitting in a place of convenience and compromise. I will encourage you to break out of that and enter into your location of inheritance and assignment. No matter what it will cost, you should do so. We should always live life on the cutting edge of complete obedience to God's Word by passing through the narrow gate of inconvenience (Matthew 7:13–14).

Deceitfulness

Moses highlighted the deceitfulness of Pharaoh's dealings as Pharaoh reneged on many prior promises and agreements he had made (Exodus 8:29). Jesus told us about the father of lies (John 8:44). He said there was no truth in him. The exact cunning nature we saw in Genesis 3 has not changed, and it continues to weave a deceptive web around those who will succumb to it.

Lies are generally connected and layered to form webs of deceit. When you meet someone who lies habitually, you tend to find out quickly that their whole life is often a falsehood, with many lies compounded together. It is difficult even to find a shroud of truth. Equally, this sounds like Satan's resume. He locks in with one lie and continues to lace every other experience with the bait of even more lies.

Truth can only emanate from a source of truth. Truth cannot originate from a source of lies.

Moses could not trust Pharaoh's words, given his previous encounters. There was a constant back-and-forth as Pharaoh would undo his earlier promises on a whim, depending on the power context he found himself. When he was under pressure through one of the judgments made by Moses, he readily made promises

(Exodus 8:8), but when there was some respite, where Pharaoh thought he regained the upper hand. His heart hardened again in pride, and he did not keep his previous promises (Exodus 8:15).

It was like trying to capture a slippery snake.

Stubbornness

We have all heard the familiar adage of a stubborn problem. This great description sounds like the experience Moses faced with Pharaoh. Pharaoh's heart hardened many times after Moses made a request. Afterward, an unwavering resolve would set in, and he would not relent from his position. Like Pharaoh, Satan only responds to power, forcing him to submit his position.

For some long-standing problems to give way, action must backup negotiation with words. You would have thought that four hundred and thirty years in bondage by Israel would be enough satisfaction for any wicked king like Pharaoh. The depth of spiritual wickedness and unyielding nature of ancient bondages often perplexes those with a sheep-like, flexible nature.

To let the children of Israel go free would have meant the end of a multi-generational system of bondage. It would have challenged the Egyptians' future and would be difficult to recover from. A power structure of subjugation kept the Egyptians as taskmasters and the children of Israel enslaved (Exodus 5:6–19).

The unrest the children of Israel experienced as a result of their bondage caused a cry for freedom to come to the ears of Jehovah Sabaoth (Exodus 2:23). A prophet, Moses, was dispatched as a deliverer to bring them out after four hundred and thirty years of bondage. He was sent by the hand of an angel, who appeared to him in the burning bush encounter (Acts 7:35). This angel brought them out with the outstretched hand of the Lord and showed them signs and wonders (Acts 7:36).

We must expect the same for our lives. We must expect the Lord to bring our families and us out of any area of challenge and limitation with signs and wonders.

Some of us may be experiencing what may seem like insurmountable spiritual roadblocks and challenges in life. Often those challenges did not come in a day, so sometimes, we can be very naive in thinking we can also eradicate them in one day. In the same way, a stubborn squatter never lets a landlord off the hook easily. So a persistent spiritual problem can also prove unyielding. The spiritual problem, like the squatter, intends to cause as much havoc as possible, standing on every legal ground until the enforcing law agents evict them by the force of the law. From this perspective, we can observe some of the multi-generational spiritual battles we may encounter.

The law we use as believers comes from the Bible. As we reflect on the promises of God to us, we come before Him—the Judge—with our petitions in prayer according to His law (Luke 18:1–8).

To go to the heavenly law courts, we must understand the law and the basis of our case. We do this by saturating our hearts with those promises denied us. We must then join our petitions with our groundbreaking Advocate Himself. Our Advocate is called Jesus Christ, the righteous. His blood represents us, which permits Him to act on behalf of those covenanted to Him by their salvation commitment (1 John 2:1). Our opponent in court is called the accuser of our brethren (Revelations 12:10).

Rebellion never accepts the law until enforced. The enforcing agents in the Kingdom of Light are the angels of God that obey His word (Psalm 103:20).

We must bring the light of the promises of God into every dark area of spiritual challenge we experience in our lives: death, disease, delay, loss, frustration, disappointment, depression, and more (Psalm 119:130). These are all contrary to the promises of life, health, advancement, prosperity, freedom, expectation, and a sound mind in God's Word (John 10:10, 3 John 2, Psalm 1:3, John 8:36, Psalm 62:5, Isaiah 26:3).

Every stubborn problem will yield to the power of God by His sent word (Psalm 107:20). As we declare those words, the angels can partner with us in enforcing them.

Your Little Ones

In Exodus 10:10–11, Pharaoh tries to impose another limitation on Israel: he tells them to leave their little ones behind.

Their little ones, or children, speak of their legacy. The same dramatic power struggle is faced by many Christians today with very high stakes. We can achieve worldly success only if we leave our little ones behind.

In the same way, Moses insisted that the little ones would not be left behind. We also must insist that we will not leave our children behind; instead, we will raise them in the way of the Lord, teaching and training them in His ways. We must ensure they are not limited like we may have been in our generation and empower them to freely express God's fullness in their generation.

Our children are for signs and wonders on the earth (Isaiah 8:18). They must carry the generational blessing due to them through the sacrifices of their parents, who were willing to confront the stronghold of limitation.

What is at stake here is compromise—a compromise of a short-term gain for long-term failure. It is a compromise on investment in our children's education for the short-term gain of material possessions. We compromise on devoting time to reading the Bible, studying, and praying with them to establish lifelong spiritual disciplines. All of this is for the short-term gain of more time on our hands to get ahead in our careers.

Finally, we compromise on manners and correction to instill a Godly character in them as parents (Proverbs 3:11). We do so for the short-term gain of wanting them to like us and wanting to be their friends.

Livestock and Herds

The other limitation Pharaoh tried to impose on the children of Israel concerned leaving their livestock behind (Exodus 10:24). What he demanded constituted a calculated form of restriction on their resources and affected what they could offer as part of their sacrifice to God.

When we walk with God, giving a sacrifice to Him is a deliberate action to demonstrate our trust and thankfulness for His provision. When we understand that every blessing we receive comes from God, it seems only fitting that we give Him a token of appreciation for what He has already given us. Every sacrifice, irrespective of size, is important to God, as Jesus showed with the widow and the two mites (Mark 12:41–44). Giving is more a test of our hearts and priorities; it is not about the amount.

Our best gift and sacrifice should deliberately be for the church. The church belongs to God (Matthew 16:18). The gift is to God and not any man or human institution.

We cannot love without giving, and we will struggle to give without loving. If our love is limited, then our giving will also be limited.

We need to see poverty as a curse, as it is clearly described in Deuteronomy 28. It is not about the family you were born in, the school or university you went to, or the privileges you lacked. It is about God and His blessing. The blessing of the Lord makes us rich and adds no sorrow (Proverbs 10:22). The unchanging Word is not dependent on any other baggage we happen to bring into life.

When we focus so much on our disadvantages, we diminish the power available in God, Who can override them with His blessing.

When blessed, we have abundant resources to give to every good work (2 Corinthians 9:8). When we are under the restriction of poverty, there is a limitation to our giving, which is an act of sacrifice (Philippians 4:18).

A limitation on our giving places a lid on our expression of love.

Despite all the different limitations Pharoah tried to place in their paths, God still delivered Israel from them all.

Their total freedom meant they could record a song of deliverance in Exodus 15. We also can believe God for complete liberation as many testimonies and songs emanate from our stories of freedom—the same way it did with the children of Israel.

CHAPTER THREE   ROADBLOCKS

My Faith Prayer

Lord, I trust You to turn every obstacle in my path into a pathway for my destiny.

Thus says the LORD, who makes a way in the sea
And a path through the mighty waters,
Who brings forth the chariot and horse,
The army and the power
(They shall lie down together, they shall not rise;
They are extinguished, they are quenched like a wick):
"Do not remember the former things,
Nor consider the things of old.
Behold, I will do a new thing,
Now it shall spring forth;
Shall you not know it?
I will even make a road in the wilderness
And rivers in the desert.
(Isaiah 43:16–19, NKJV)

My Relentless Faith Testimonies

Record here the many ways God has amazed you as you relentlessly stretched your faith.

CHAPTER THREE   ROADBLOCKS

Chapter Four

Shadow Fighting

A boxer fighting an opponent is the picture of a real fight. Any other view will be a shadow of the real—in essence, a counterfeit. The image of someone shadow boxing or shadow fighting falls into this category because someone is fighting a shadow of the real opponent.

The shadow fighter is fighting something that is not real.

If you are not fighting the real thing, then you are using up a lot of sweat and energy fighting something which will never give you victory. There are no belts of accomplishment to be won from shadow fighting.

This same analogy applies spiritually. Imagine waging war against something spiritually that is not your real opponent. You are praying hard and fasting. You are confessing the Word and the promises of God. Despite all your efforts, your "spiritual blows" are landing on the wrong target. The shadow fighting war ends in futility: all pain but no gain.

I wanted to start with a crystal-clear picture of what this chapter is all about. As is often quoted, a picture speaks louder than a thousand words. With this vivid imagery in mind, let us step through this chapter and observe the different counterfeit fights we may have unknowingly engaged in.

Fighting People

As the timeless adage goes, your mother-in-law is not the enemy! God bless all mothers-in-law! The Apostle Paul lets us into a critical insight when he tells us our wrestling in our spiritual war is not against flesh and blood. It is not against people. Instead, it is against principality, powers, rulers of the darkness of this age, and spiritual hosts of wickedness in the heavenly places

(Ephesians 6:12). These are all spiritual forces, not human beings.

Suppose we expend all our energy and efforts fighting people. In that case, we step out of the commandment of love and experience darkness (1 John 2:11). Our calling means loving everyone, including our enemies (Matthew 5:43–47). Loving our enemies perfects us (Matthew 5:48).

Instead of landing our spiritual punches on the actual target, we could be fighting naturally as one who beats the air (1 Corinthians 9:26). We could expend a lot of spiritual energy on petty squabbles, political infighting, unforgiveness, and offense, ultimately bringing division.

Or we could take a deep breath and take it a notch higher, into the spiritual battleground. On this battleground, we can pray in the spirit and allow the Holy Spirit to empty the venom of offense from our bodies before we let the sun go down on our anger (Ephesians 4:26).

The Holy Spirit is great at trawling through the events of the day alongside us if we permit Him to, shining the light of identification on the areas where we need repentance. Maybe events sparked our anger, pride, stubbornness, and the digging in of our heels. Others provoked outbursts of wrath as we flew off the handle. There may have been incidents of lying with all shades of the truth rather than the whole truth. We may have engaged in displays of competition, covetousness, and unbridled ambition. The list goes on and on.

Our prayers could be animated and engaging if we focused more on repentance—"I am sorry" instead of the endless desires of our hearts demanded in prayer—"This is what I want." God's grace remains available to help us in our repentance journey of humility (2 Chronicles 7:14).

We must always take on an attitude of humility that bursts at the seams with daily mental notes of where we could do better tomorrow.

Equally, I pray we can rip up our long list of grievances with others at the end of each day and have repentance-soaked tears on a blank sheet of paper readily waiting for the next day. Everyday love gladly brings out a fresh new sheet of mercy paper for others (Matthew 5:7). Love keeps no record of wrong (1 Corinthians 13:5).

Fighting Seasons

Have you heard of someone swimming against the tide? Ordinarily, a person will swim with the tide by finding out which way the tide is going and aligning themselves accordingly. But one who swims against the tide has decided not to bother with that. They have chosen instead to dive in and are now almost fighting the direction of the waves. It is the same way when we see someone walking up an escalator going down. It would be easier to take the escalator going up instead.

These two everyday examples provide powerful insights into what it means to fight a season. The tide of wisdom is knowing what season we are in and responding appropriately.

Are we trying to harvest in a season meant for sowing? Are we dressed in summer clothes when the chilly air suggests we are in winter? Are we pushing for a breakthrough in a season of preparation where no doors will open?

CHAPTER FOUR   SHADOW FIGHTING

There is a timing to everything under the sun, as the wise man Solomon in the Bible tells us (Ecclesiastes 3:1–8). There is a time to sow, and there is a time to reap. There is a time and a season for everything in life.

Usually, all new working parents are encouraged to take some time off after the birth of their child. Culture understands that bonding takes priority over work in that season. Hopefully, they recognize this and take up the opportunity instead of fighting the tide by going into the office the next day.

I spent the early part of my Christian journey operating without much wisdom. I was running with a lot of zeal but not much wisdom. I was fighting on so many levels. I find it exhausting even thinking about that past season of my life. I was trying to open doors, which, in hindsight, would never have opened in that season. I was trying to accelerate things that needed time to grow and mature.

Now, I very much pick my "fights." I ask the Lord first to help me understand what season I am in currently. Once I know, it determines my focus of study, prayers, even the songs I sing! It also influences all other activities I give most of my attention to during that season.

Also connected to seasons, over time, I have learned two crucial principles around focus and momentum, which I will discuss later (in Chapter 9, which is on distractions).

My season determines the areas I go into with my faith. My season also defines the boundaries I push in faith.

Fighting Day and Night

We must also understand the cycle of the season we are in. Within each season, there are also cycles. In winter, it gets darker earlier, and the days are shorter. In summer, the days are longer, and it gets darker a lot later, sometimes well into the night.

Jesus used the day and night cycle to describe a period of opportunity He had to complete His assignment, which was the day (John 9:4).

Some things we achieve by walking through the park on a summer morning will be better done then than on a frosty winter morning while wrapped up snugly at home.

We must understand the most opportune time for accomplishing a task. I write for extended periods in the spring and summer, especially during the day. The words just seem to flow better, and even my keyboard responds in harmony as I type. This is in contrast to winter, late at night, when the noise sounds more like a banging on my keyboard with long pauses as I try to fill the endless blank pages.

Apart from not fighting seasons, we must also learn not to fight the cycle we are in within a season. The key to managing seasons and cycles is our ability to recognize them and respond appropriately to what we have recognized.

Fighting Emotions

Part of victory in life is also about understanding our temperament. Most people are not very productive when they are angry. So we must do our utmost to hold back ourselves and minimize our outbursts of anger. We need to understand our negative emotional triggers and protect our productivity from them.

However, on the cusp of some good news we have just heard, our mood is lifted, and we have a sense that we are ready to climb any mountain. Instead of holding back, this is when we permit ourselves to release the dams of positive emotional triggers, unleashing ourselves to accelerate our productivity exponentially.

Similarly, studying the Word of God and prayer flows more easily after we have just basked in God's presence in worship. Dancing comes easier after we have just listened to someone share a miraculous testimony.

After experiencing some form of loss, we tend to feel deflated and lackluster with our emotions. Natural circumstances do play a part in determining our feelings. Our choices and actions also play a role.

However, as we mature in Christ, we understand that the Word of God becomes the most significant regulator of our emotions. How can you count it all joy when we fall into various trials and tribulations (Romans 5:3)? We can because it does not stop there; it says the testing of our faith produces patience (James 1:2–3) and hope. It also says the Holy Spirit pours out the love of God into our hearts (Romans 5:4–5).

CHAPTER FOUR   SHADOW FIGHTING

Amazing! One of the many reasons why I love the Word of God. These are not ordinary words spun differently depending on the speaker, but they are spirit-filled words that inspire hope and encouragement. They breathe new life into tired problems. They give us the strength to go again, even after countless setbacks. They carry us on through thick and thin, through difficulty and through pressure, until we enter the open space of peace it creates.

Fighting Destiny

Whenever I ponder that God never consults us before He writes our destinies, it always proves very instructive to me. It is an act of His will, not an act of democracy. I am so glad He does not consult with us. How could I ever have fathomed the story of my life, having now only literally scratched the surface of it? And it has only been light and superficial scratching from the volumes of books already written about me and wrapped up in the carrier womb of destiny.

My pastor always says destiny is about discovery. What a wise statement! That is the blessing of having a pastor; one priceless gem uttered into studious ears can change your life course forever.

I have discovered recently that the Lord only pays for what He orders. Let us unpack that heavy statement and bring it down to a movie scene we have often found ourselves in as the lead actor.

You go into a restaurant and order that delicious meal you have already prepared mentally in your mind. However, what shows up is a paltry, unappetizing and different version of what you expected. What do we do? We politely say to the waiter—well, I hope we do it reasonably and with grace. If you are a Brit, the request is likely to be in quiet tones of understatement, almost apologizing for raising the issue. Decorating the central part of your message with an "I am extremely sorry" thrown in before and afterward.

Whichever way you deliver the news, it remains unequivocal: "This is not what I ordered." Most likely, a table mix-up becomes unraveled as you confirm what you ordered with the frazzled waiter.

In the same way, we would not usually overlook such a mistake and eat the wrong order or even pay for it. I have found that our destiny is too precious to Our Lord for Him to change His mind on what He ordered.

God may have called you like Moses to be a deliverer of a nation numbering millions. Also, like Moses, God may be preparing you to be the answer to the prayers of a group under oppression that have come up as a flailing cry to the Lord's ears. It would be best not to shortchange this for something else.

Destinies are connected and related. When Moses received the commission for his assignment, every man, woman, and child's future lay connected to his response. That deduction may seem obvious, but it is worth restating. Similarly, the Greatest Spiritual Architect of Moses's life and our lives understands that every detail has a meaning and an intention. No element is an afterthought.

Imagine if another millennial deliverer decided that rather than fulfill her original assignment, she would instead focus all her spiritual energy on becoming a superstar musician. She decides that the lure of fame and fortune is much more appealing than being a deliverer. No matter how hard the pull to become a musician may be, this deliverer would still be fighting against her spiritual destiny.

Fighting God

The final fight we do not want to fight is one against God. Thank God for Prophet Jonah. He has become the poster child for what not to do. We look at Jonah's life and see what we consider an extreme example of fighting God in disobedience. However, grains of Jonah's traits remain dusted through most of our lives. Ours may not be on the same scale as Jonah's; we tend to reason. But if we look closely, we have also disagreed with God on things like Jonah. Can the clay argue with the potter, as Jeremiah wondered (Jeremiah 18:1–11)?

We can be fans of God in certain areas of our lives. But we may wish we held the pen in other places as we see ourselves having much better ideas about our story, especially when we suffer. We see this when Paul pleads with the Lord over that painful thorn for its removal. The answer was: "My Grace will fill up what is required to allow you to endure the pain from this thorn which is difficult" (2 Corinthians 12:7–10).

I remember many circumstances where I have been raw with emotions from a thorn that I endured patiently. My soul recoiled from the inconvenience, the pain, and the trauma of this foreign obstruction in my life. It was like a grate on my flesh.

Paul could say I am what I am by the grace of God (1 Corinthians 15:10) because this same grace had helped him endure this thorn in his life.

The thorn is usually a sensitive area in our lives—one we could have cried over in anguish. We generally do not want many people getting too close to us and starting to peer into this area. It is that place seemingly off-limits in our lives, where the mere mention of this area raises alarm bells in our emotions.

God used a kind and loving friend to speak to me about my thorn. She casually mentioned on a phone call that the Lord gave her a revelation and asked her to pray for me in a particular area. I had not realized I had built such an emotional wall around this area until she spoke. As soon as she mentioned the words, I felt incredibly vulnerable. I sidestepped the issue by covering my pain.

Like the woman with the issue of blood hiding a lot of pain under the garment of clothing (Mark 5:25–34), I was equally hurting but still desperate for a solution. I hid my desperation on my issue. Like the woman with the issue of blood, I felt I could only be genuinely vulnerable on my level of distress with the Master. Only He could understand that I had exhausted all my resources trying to solve the problem, but it seemed to grow worse.

As I type these words on this early morning, I sense that these words may bring deliverance to many. Even as I write this, there is a tightness and a surrender of the pain to My Lord Jesus. Only He can approach the stench of the grave to call Lazarus forth (John 11:43). Only He can touch the leper in his area of shame (Matthew 8:1–3). Only He can remove the reproach from the barren womb (Luke 1:24–25).

In each case, He never uncovers them by sharing their story for them; instead, He waits for them to share their testimony of victory themselves. As they share their testimony, they experience an emotional deliverance alongside their spiritual one. The emotions attached to any indignity they suffered released in that one precious act.

Real ministry comes when wounded healers arise. Out of the pain they have suffered, they are now willing to incubate the pain of others in intercession. In the place they also scrabbled for help, they become the helping hands for others, protecting them from feelings of helplessness. They carry the burden of others willingly because, through their journey, the Lord has built in them the capacity to do so.

My Faith Prayer

Lord, help me not to fight people you have placed in my life to be a source of blessing. Let Your love overwhelm every fight happening in my relationships.

Love never fails. But whether there are prophecies, they will fail; whether there are tongues, they will cease; whether there is knowledge, it will vanish away.
(1 Corinthians 13:8, NKJV)

CHAPTER FOUR SHADOW FIGHTING

My Relentless Faith Testimonies

Record here the many ways God has amazed you as you relentlessly stretched your faith.

Chapter Five

Big Bully

The "God" kind of faith is an unwavering faith that keeps going despite tragic circumstances. We see this in the Book of Job. When the *Book of Job* is mentioned, a certain air of despair can often descend on our minds.

However, we must look at the whole *Book of Job* in its entirety to get the whole message.

The whole message is that at the end of the book, Job got back everything he had lost and more, physically and spiritually. Why do I say *more* spiritually? Through his experience, he gained a more profound knowledge of God. I believe that intimate knowledge was priceless to Job.

Faith always triumphs over circumstances, no matter how tragic those circumstances may be. Out of the other side also comes a fire-tested and enduring faith (1 Peter 1:7).

Tragic events also reveal the heart of those around us, as Job found out. His friends did not sit with him in his sorrow as he expected but instead started pointing accusing fingers at him. Even his wife suggested he should curse God.

How demoralizing this must have been for poor Job. In the crucible of a tragedy, those you thought would hold you up by their faith reveal they are really on a different journey to you, and theirs is dictated solely by the circumstances of life.

The tragic events only showed what was already there—as the shallow nature of their present level of unbelief is exposed. Often, like in *The Parable of the Sower*, it is revealed that the word of faith has not yet found the right level of depth in their life, so circumstances and tragedies can quickly shake it loose (Matthew 13:5,20–21).

Job's story is exemplary because it shows us that tragedy is not determined by how righteous you are. Jesus repeated this lesson in His commentary on the men of Siloam, who also experienced tragedy (Luke 13:4).

Job's Narrative

Job's idyllic life at the start of this book in the Bible is not too dissimilar to the front cover splash on the pages of a luxury magazine. He was living the good life. It was so good that his children's favorite hobby was throwing parties. They were hanging out together at every opportunity (Job 1:4). We do not know of any other activities they were engaged in during their short lives (Job 1:19).

Job regularly covered his children by sacrificing on their behalf for any behavior which may have grieved God (Job 1:5). Sadly, this is what many parents are still doing today all across the globe.

That was until tragedy struck on that fateful day, and Job lost everything. His appearance changed dramatically; he wore a torn robe and shaved his head to depict the disaster he had suffered (Job 1:20).

Even in his turmoil, Job did a very unusual thing. He worshipped God, as we see in Job 1:20–21 (NKJV).

> *Then Job arose, tore his robe, and shaved his head;*
> *and he fell to the ground and worshipped.*
> *And he said:*
> *"Naked I came from my mother's womb,*
> *And naked shall I return there.*
> *The LORD gave, and the LORD has taken away;*
> *Blessed be the name of the LORD."*

Tragedy did not diminish who God was in Job's eyes. However, this was not the end of Job's affliction. Not only did he lose his children, but his body was also afflicted.

The depths of his grief could be seen in Job 2:12–13 when his three friends no longer recognized him after his series of tragedies.

> *And when they raised their eyes from afar, and did not recognize him, they lifted their voices and wept; and each one tore his robe and sprinkled dust on his head toward heaven.*

CHAPTER FIVE BIG BULLY

So they sat down with him on the ground seven days and seven nights, and no one spoke a word to him, for they saw that his grief was very great.

Job's situation became a hopeless case that defied explanation. He became an outcast amongst his friends, whose lives continued seemingly uninterrupted.

The following chapters in Job's life found him searching for God amidst tragedy. His soul could only be comforted by God. He suffered physically and emotionally with the burden of this tragedy. He started to ask questions of which there was no earlier record. He began to ponder life and its fragility. He began to express his grief.

Those who should have continued to surround him with words of comfort did not do so. His only refuge was God. Tragedy forced him to press into a deep place in God.

Going beyond the superficial platitudes to honest discourse brought new authenticity to Job's relationship with God.

In many chapters, God just listened to Job. He gave him the precious gift of listening, allowing him to pour out his heart without interruption. Job poured his bitterness, anger, and despair into a sea of safety with God. We do not serve a God who is so weak; He cannot handle difficult questions or challenges from us.

The *Book of Job* allows us to see God as a caring father instead of a judge. God gave Job time to process his emotions and thoughts. He allowed Job time for the rawness of his hurt, loss, and disappointment to be expressed.

Trusted with Adversity

During his crisis, Job made a startling statement in response to his wife's suggestion that he should curse God (Job 2:10).

> *But he said to her, "You speak as one of the foolish women speaks. Shall we indeed accept good from God, and shall we not accept adversity?" In all this, Job did not sin with his lips.*
>
> Job 2:10 (NKJV)

CHAPTER FIVE BIG BULLY

Can we be trusted with adversity? Can we be trusted to handle adversity without cursing God? Job did not curse God throughout his challenges, but he cursed the day of his birth (Job 3:1). Later, he had to repent from this curse (Job 42:1–6).

Like Job, in the years after the global reset of 2020, years in which many individuals, families, and nations have suffered tragedies, let us resist the temptation to curse God and ourselves.

God was confident when speaking to Satan about Job. There was an assurance that Job would not step over that line of lifting his voice to curse God (Job 1:8–12, Job 2:3–6). He would not curse his source. Ultimately, God trusted that this righteous man would not forget who he was.

No matter how desperate our circumstances, let us resist the lies, deception, and trickery intended to get us to start on this slippery slope to destruction. As David exclaimed, it is better to fall into God's hand than into the hand of man (2 Samuel 24:14).

Loosing the Bonds of Oppression

Tragedy and difficult circumstances in life can bring a bond of oppression to our lives. This oppression can range in its manifestation.

It could start from the oppression of our bodies through sickness. Later, the oppression of our minds and emotions through anguish from a siege of tragedies, one after the other. We may even experience the oppression of our destinies through the illegitimate authority of others who spoke against us. Finally, we may suffer the oppression of our identity if we trade in our high calling of destiny for a substitute at a lower rung.

The Lord speaks of a fast: a kind of fast that looses the bonds of wickedness and lets the oppressed go free (Isaiah 58:6).

> *"Is this not the fast that I have chosen:*
> *To loose the bonds of wickedness,*
> *To undo the heavy burdens,*
> *To let the oppressed go free,*
> *And that you break every yoke?*
>
> Isaiah 58:6 (NKJV)

CHAPTER FIVE BIG BULLY

The cry for justice or mercy is one that God cannot ignore. Jesus highlights this in *The Parable of the Persistent Widow* (Luke 18:1–8).

We can be like the persistent widow, joining the chorus from earth to heaven, a chorus crying out night and day for deliverance. Many are crying out for deliverance from the bonds of oppression for their families and many others. God shall avenge them.

> *And shall God not avenge His own elect who cry out day and night to Him, though He bears long with them?*
> *"I tell you that He will avenge them speedily. Nevertheless, when the Son of Man comes, will He really find faith on the earth?"*
> Luke 18:7–8 (NKJV)

The Lord expects to find faith on the earth when He returns. He will seek a faithful remnant of believers who have been registering their voices in heaven, night and day, crying out for justice for the oppressed.

They will refuse to be silent until God establishes His peace over the earth.

> *I have set watchmen on your walls, O Jerusalem;*
> *They shall never hold their peace day or night.*
> *You who make mention of the LORD, do not keep silent,*
> *And give Him no rest till He establishes*
> *And till He makes Jerusalem a praise in the earth.*
>
> Isaiah 62:6–7 (NKJV)

The scripture above presents a license not to be polite in our prayers, as we recognize that our words are not harmless chatter easily ignored but instead, our prayers sound the ringing cries of a siren that cause unrest in heaven.

In the *Book of Exodus,* in the Old Testament, we can also see that God listens to the cry of the oppressed, and He always sends an answer of deliverance (Exodus 3:7–8).

We need the verdict from heaven on our earthly circumstances. We have the right to take our case to the heavenly courts, bring the judgment from heaven back to earth, and establish it.

CHAPTER FIVE BIG BULLY

The voice of the accuser of the brethren can no longer sound louder than the voice of the saints in the heavenly courts, especially when we have the Great Advocate representing us (1 John 2:1). We welcome a season where the backlogs of accusatory cases against God's children become cleared out of the heavenly courts with a swift "Case dismissed!" statement.

Angel of Deliverance

God did not send Moses alone on his assignment of deliverance for Israel. An angel of deliverance was also sent with him to execute judgment.

> *"This Moses whom they rejected, saying, 'Who made you a ruler and a judge?' is the one God sent to be a ruler and a deliverer by the hand of the Angel who appeared to him in the bush.*
>
> Acts 7:35 (NKJV)

We need supernatural assistance in our deliverance journey from any challenge, and God never lets us down. His angels of deliverance are raring to go. Just speak the word they are saying, and in a flash, they are there to execute the judgment. God's words never return to Him without accomplishing their assignment (Isaiah 55:11).

We see this when the unsheathed sword appears in the Angel of the Lord's hands to protect Israel from a money-hungry and disobedient prophet. The Angel was there to ensure the rebellious prophet only spoke God's Word to Israel and not what Israel's enemy had hired him to say (Numbers 22:23–35).

Warfare for deliverance and victory ensues. These are not messenger angels bringing good news, but warrior angels dispatched for breakthrough (Daniel 10:13).

CHAPTER FIVE   BIG BULLY

My Faith Prayer

Lord, help me not to allow fear to have the upper hand in my life as I surrender all my fear battles to You.

---

*The LORD will fight for you,
and you shall hold your peace."
(Exodus 14:14, NKJV)*

My Relentless Faith Testimonies

Record here the many ways God has amazed you as you relentlessly stretched your faith.

CHAPTER FIVE   BIG BULLY

Chapter Six

Failure Hero

This chapter has been called the *Failure Hero*. We do not often see those two words together, failure and hero, but as we go through this chapter, we will better understand why we have the magnificent coupling.

Failure is part of the fragility that makes us human. Each one of us has failed at some point in our lives. We have feelings for a reason as an outlet and release for failure, disappointment, and loss. Failure, if not dealt with properly, can lead to frustration. However, a failure hero uses failures to their advantage.

Failure forces us to confront four perspectives that ultimately benefit us: complacency, humility, compassion, and submission. Now, we look at each in turn. What you are about to hear will be great for your soul.

Complacency

Israel became complacent when they went into a war, assuming that the ark in their camp guaranteed them victory. We see this in 1 Samuel 4:3–11.

After their first defeat in 1 Samuel 4:1–2, which cost Israel four thousand men in their army, they stopped short in their questioning to uncover the real reason for their defeat. Instead, they turned to the ark as their sure solution.

> *And when the people had come into the camp, the elders of Israel said, "Why has the LORD defeated us today before the Philistines? Let us bring the ark of covenant of the LORD from Shiloh to us, that when it comes among us it may save us from the hand of our enemies."*
>
> *So the people sent to Shiloh, that they might bring from there the ark of the covenant of the LORD of hosts, who dwells between the cherubim. And the*

> *two sons of Eli, Hophni and Phinehas, were there with the ark of the covenant of God.*
> *And when the ark of the LORD came into the camp, all Israel shouted so loudly that the earth shook.*
>
> 1 Samuel 4:3–5 (NKJV)

I recently went through an experience of failure, and it allowed me to understand my journey around complacency better.

My complacency journey started after a flash of victory concerning a series of challenging presentations I had to deliver. With these early successes under my belt, I decided to go head-on, full of faith, into the final round of work-related presentations.

However, in hindsight, I had not prepared or protected myself from every possible scenario which could have gone wrong. I had not practiced how I would respond in each case. I had not tested all the equipment I needed to fulfill this final set of presentations.

We see parallels in the account we read in 1 Samuel 4:3–5. The Israelites also had not practiced or rehearsed their spiritual military drills and war plans. They had not gone through the introspection of searching over their sinful lives, patterns, and lifestyles. They had not gone through the prerequisite of national repentance before entering the battle. They had leaned too much on the certainty of the ark alone to give them victory.

Sin is very deceitful. It is especially true of hidden sins like pride, which fuels complacency. In the same way Israel did, I had leaned too much on a revelation of victory based on previous successes before entering my final round for presentations. I can confirm that pride was indeed responsible for my failure.

However, this realization only came after failure, when I retrospectively examined my life, patterns, and lifestyle, looking for sin.

Often, when we mention sin, most minds immediately jump to the outward type of sin. However, the inward corruption of pride or unforgiveness is often more dangerous. They easily lull us into a false sense of security, causing us to believe everything is all right on the bridge of our outward lives. Meanwhile, underneath the bridge lie destructive mindsets, patterns, and lifestyles that repulse God's power and grace.

Thank God; He loves me so much that He uses circumstances to awaken me to my spiritual reality. Then, if I am willing to accept the invitation to this spiritual awakening, I can take immediate and consistent action for permanent freedom. During this awakening, I welcome the new patterns emerging from a renewed mindset, which lead to new cycles of behavior and action.

If we look at it more closely, failure is a very precious gift from God. I have learned more from my failures in life than my successes.

Would the Apostle Paul have written most of the New Testament had he not failed woefully in the early part of his life as a persecutor of the church? In failure, Paul learned about God's grace. God's grace is also available to us today wherever we have received defeat. Do not waste your failures; let them propel you to greater heights in your walk with God.

In the Nigerian Yoruba language, my full name, "Olufunmbi," which I shorten, means "God gave me to birth." All my books started nicely with God-given titles and ideas, but ultimately they were birthed in the pain of failure. Birthing remains an excruciating process. I have learned not to waste my painful failures but to channel them into birthing something great for God.

If I can do it, so can you. It took me two years to write my first book. I released three books on my next outing, and now I am going for more.

The force of your pain brings the contractions that release a miracle into your life. Out of something so messy as failure, we can experience the immense beauty of character growth.

Also, with each birthing process, you learn things you could never experience until you had been through the birthing journey. What you learn through the experience helps to quicken your delivery next time.

Through my painful experience of failure, I learned everything I present to you, dear reader, in this chapter of the book.

Humility

Humility, simply put, acknowledges the fact that we are not God. All of us will fall short at some point in our lives. That realization keeps us in check of not getting too carried away with ourselves and becoming blinded to God and His sovereignty. When we are full of ourselves, we are empty of God. When we are full of God, we are devoid of ourselves. I know which of these two options I would prefer. One, even though it may be full, sounds very hollow.

I now understand what Paul meant when he said he would rather boast in his weaknesses that the grace of God may rest on him (2 Corinthians 12:9–10). In essence, what he may have been requoting in another way was: God resists the proud but gives grace to the humble (James 4:6).

We can lose our lives in humility to gain it again in God.

Today, you can decide to wrap humility as a blanket around your life. In doing so, you are allowing it to keep you in the warmth of God's presence, where you find rest and safety from the blistering cold of pride.

You may decide to pray this regularly. "Lord, lace my words with Your threads of humility and kindness. Let the beauty of Your humble and kind love emerge from the tapestry of my life."

Compassion

Failure also teaches us compassion. I think of Moses before and after the incident that changed his destiny.

Moses was a crown prince in Pharaoh's house. He had all the privilege and background of being raised in the palace (Exodus 2:10). He most likely rubbed shoulders with the learned, wealthy, and influential while growing up. He would probably have had the satisfaction of immediately seeing all his whims, desires, and commands fulfilled.

However, inside the spiritual genes of Moses, the future judge, prophet, and deliverer of Israel, lay a desire for justice.

Events unfolded on that fateful day when Moses walked into the midst of injustice as an Israelite received mistreatment from an Egyptian (Exodus 2:11).

The desire for justice struck an immediate chord as Moses took the law into his own hands. He became judge and jury before his appointed time. He resorted to an illegal method of murder to correct an injustice (Exodus 2:12).

What followed was a huge blow and damage to his reputation, as others now recognized him as a murderer (Exodus 2:14). Moses now began his journey of hiddenness in the wilderness. He was running away from himself and his failure (Exodus 2:15). A crown prince became a shepherd looking after sheep in the wilderness for forty long years of testing. In these forty years, Moses became an afterthought. He lost all his bravado and confidence.

How do we know this? We see this when we meet him again at the burning bush experience with the Angel of God (Exodus 3:2–3). When heaven called out, asking, "Who can we send as a deliverer to Egypt to redress the injustice and cry of the people from the cruelty of bondage?" Moses did not put his hand up (Exodus 3:11). Instead, he gave every excuse in the book as to why he was not qualified for the assignment (Exodus 4:1, Exodus 4:10, Exodus 4:13).

CHAPTER SIX FAILURE HERO

Have you ever had the experience of emails coming through to you that you thought had been addressed to the wrong person? It's a case of mistaken identity.

Moses' response made it clear that he believed God had dropped an email in the wrong inbox. He essentially said, "Lord, I think you meant to address this email to a mighty warrior who has the strength to deliver a whole nation. You missed it, Lord! You sent it to the wrong email address. No person fits that description at this address. My email address is Moses@stutterer.com. You wanted someone with @confidence.com at the end of their email address."

However, God, who created Moses, persisted. It felt almost like this was the kind of conversation going on in heaven. "Let us send him in when he gets in there with whatever aid he needs to give him confidence (Exodus 4:16). That gift I placed in him will revive. His identity as the faith leader I have called him to be will come alive and reignite again."

When Moses meets with the mirror of a cruel and stubborn leader with no reverence for God and no compassion for His people, that gift of mercy to see justice for others will arise and meet with the legitimacy of the right timing and the authority of being a sent one from God.

We see this unfold in real life as the fireworks of God's heavenly spiritual power met in a clash of titans with the earthly power of a king in Pharaoh, who mistook himself for a god.

The previous failure, Moses became the mighty spiritual deliverer willing to confront a superpower in the earth and bring the sovereignty of God's judgment to bear. He did so through the release of ten supernatural plagues.

Failure tends to broaden our hearts in compassion toward others who have also failed in life. Our experience allows us to look at them through the renewed lens of what they did with their failure.

An analogy I heard rings through in this area. Failure can either make you bitter or better. I add that failure can either make you a more compassionate leader or make you an even more terrifying leader.

Terrifying leaders are leaders who have no compassion for those they serve. Each failure from those under their leadership care is met with the cold stare of "you should have known better" instead of accompaniment through learning, recovery, and restoration.

Jesus, the Compassionate Leader, walked through those same steps of learning, recovery, and restoration with Peter after he failed abysmally on the three tests of loyalty he received. The stakes were life and death. Peter listened to the crow of the rooster announcing his "three strikes, and you are out" report back to his mind (Matthew 26:75).

Peter ran away from his leadership promise back to the wilderness of fishing (John 21:3). Jesus came and met him with the compassion of the Resurrected King (John 21:15). He walked him through the steps of first learning, then recovery, and finally restoration to his position in the church (John 21:15–19).

Submission

We return to the story of Moses. Moses became a submitted leader. He was one now under a higher authority. He only spoke the words he received. He was carefully following the protocol and script unveiled to him after each encounter with Pharaoh.

Judging a house you grew up in must have been a difficult assignment for Moses. However, Moses 2.0, when we meet him, is a different man. He became one who had died to himself and his reputation. Moses now became totally submitted to God's plan, timing, and method. He typified Lazarus, raised from the dead and walking around now in his resurrected clothes. He was the dead man in his flesh, alive again now in renewal and covenant with God.

On the morning after another harrowing experience of failure, I am writing to say I had a choice to sink into the mire of giving up or swimming. However, I realized that genuine faith is a tested faith. Real faith is a submitted faith. Faith does not deny failure. Great faith allows the truth of God's Word to override the emotion of defeat. It stares failure in the face and declares Romans 8:28.

CHAPTER SIX FAILURE HERO

> *"And we know that all things work together for good to those who love God, to those who are called according to His purpose."*
>
> Romans 8:28 (NKJV)

As most entrepreneurs know, failure can either make you or break you. Failure can never break genuine faith. It just becomes more robust when more pressure is placed on it. Was this what Jesus meant when He said whatever is born of God overcomes the world (1 John 5:4)?

The Spirit of God, which all newborn-again believers become birthed in, is a Spirit of faith. It is a Spirit, which cannot be defeated. It is an overcoming Spirit that always leads believers to triumph. Such triumph is chronicled in the *Book of Hebrews*, which contains a long history of an overcoming army that is still raising recruits today. The miraculous testimonies of believers are spectacularly evident in the Bible.

I attend a church where testimonies are shared every week before the preaching part of the service starts.

It creates an atmosphere of faith as we enter God's Word to enlighten our darkness. As we listen, our ear of faith becomes attuned to the frequency of heaven. Our ears start to pick up both the spoken word in the service and the unspoken words in the whisperings of the Holy Spirit.

The Holy Spirit knows which episode is playing in the box set season of our individual lives, giving Him the free reign to accentuate the right words. Those words always tie up with the episode we are going through right now and show us the relevant Rhema insight we desperately need to end the episode on a high note.

We spoke earlier in this chapter about Israel's first defeat against the Philistines in 1 Samuel 4:1–2. We now pick up the story again. After a second failed attempt at defeating the Philistines in 1 Samuel 4:10–11, Israel finally prepares its heart to return to God in repentance (1 Samuel 7:3–6).

After this time of national repentance, Israel subsequently experienced their much sought-after victory against the Philistines (1 Samuel 7:10–14).

CHAPTER SIX FAILURE HERO

After my brush with failure on a demanding series of work presentations, I had to deliver, which I referred to earlier in this chapter, in the section on complacency.

On my final outing, I prepared so hard. I left no stone unturned until the last minute before the final presentation. My efforts were rewarded with a spectacular and resounding result and total victory from God.

Would I have prepared so hard if I had not experienced earlier failure? Certainly not!

Having failed earlier, I had learned from my painful mistakes of overconfidence and pride, so I took a new posture of humility as I approached this second time round. Character growth had emerged from what would have been a devastating blow if I had not learned what I needed from it.

I close this chapter on the Failure Hero, re-emphasizing that failure is not the end if you choose to learn from it. Failure also eradicates complacency from our lives. It clothes us in humility, compassion, and submission. All these elements are of great value to us as we progress on our spiritual development and faith walk.

My Faith Prayer

Lord, help me to use the lessons of failure as a stepping stone to my next level of growth.

And we know that all things work together for good to those who love God, to those who are the called according to His purpose.
(Romans 8:28, NKJV)

My Relentless Faith Testimonies

Record here the many ways God has amazed you as you relentlessly stretched your faith.

_____
_____
_____
_____
_____
_____
_____
_____
_____
_____
_____
_____
_____
_____
_____
_____
_____
_____
_____
_____
_____
_____

Chapter Seven

No One Wins

Much energy would be conserved in life when we run our race and stay in our lanes. Many are running a race they should not be running. They saw a 10,000m runner and admired the grace and elegance as they ran the first lap of their race. Then they decided to jump on their track, not realizing this was only their first lap! Unknown to them, the long-distance runner has the grace of endurance to run their race to the last lap with another grace kicking in at the end called tenacity and grit.

The person who decided to jump on the track may have received the grace of burst sprinting for a 100m or

200m race. However, they are now in the wrong competition, clearly out of their depth and struggling with a particular, inevitable result looming.

Those who compete with others in their race of life end up losing on so many fronts.

Losing the Reward

When we compare ourselves to others, Christians fail to realize that we are becoming unwise (2 Corinthians 10:12). Precious time can be lost when we engage in competition. We can never win in a race we were never meant to run. Only those assigned to a race are qualified to receive a prize at the end of it (1 Corinthians 9:24–25).

It is not far-fetched to believe that heaven has a register of those meant to run in their assigned races. They will be measured and rewarded only based on their designated race. There is no prize for running in the wrong race.

Hopefully, the reality of this last statement will be the smell of coffee that wakes us up in awareness. We must arise from our slumbering sleep before we mistakenly start preparing for any form of competition.

CHAPTER SEVEN   NO ONE WINS

We see this also in *The Parable of the Talents* (Matthew 25:14–30). Each servant gave an account based on what they had received. Theirs was not to focus on what others had received but to look at how they could multiply the precious talents they had. Their commendation and reward hinged purely on what they did with what they had.

The master of these servants was specific. He knew what each was given and measured them by that yardstick.

The terminology used was quite business-like; it was about "came and settled accounts with them" (Matthew 25:19).

Their master was well qualified to determine what He chose to give each one. Like them, comparing what we have received to others should never be our focus. Our primary concern should be faithfulness and fruitfulness with what we do receive.

The commendation given to the one who had five talents and doubled it and the one who had two talents and equally doubled it (Matthew 25:21, 23) was pretty much almost identical.

"Well done, good and faithful servant; you were faithful over a few things, I will make you a ruler over many things. Enter into the joy of your lord" (Matthew 25:21).

The message is clear: it is not what you started with which matters, but what you did with it. You will only be rewarded for running your assigned race.

Losing the Joy

Jesus spoke about the joy set before him to complete His race (Hebrews 12:2). That joy was only available to Him as a reward for completing His race. This joy speaks of total fulfillment despite requiring the greatest sacrifice ever made for eternity.

Jesus could carry His cross because it was part of His race. He also received divine grace and strength in the place of prayer because it was part of His assignment (Luke 22:41–44). Heaven's resources were available to

Him when He called because He was walking in obedience and following God's will (John 5:30).

As the end of His life on earth approached, the cup Jesus was about the drink from was a costly cup. He could pass on the cup, but He chose not to. He decided to surrender His will to the Father's will (Matthew 26:39–42).

He chose to sacrifice instead of compromise so His joy would be complete.

Have you ever watched a running event in athletics where the competition has been extremely intense? In that case, you can relate to the scene when you see the winner cross over the finish line first after throwing in everything but the kitchen sink into their race. There is usually a look of total exhaustion as they collapse, spent from their exertions. At the same time, there is always a look of absolute joy. Unspeakable joy is written all over their faces.

Their satisfaction is derived from legitimacy and fulfillment.

For Jesus, following God's will involved what we would characterize today as extreme suffering, rejection, ridicule, and sacrifice. However, that was His race: to drink from the cup of crucifixion for the sake of the eternal harvest, which continues till today. That sounds like good news to me! Thank God for the obedience of the Messiah!

No Winner

There is no winner with the spirit of competition. It is a spirit that is never satisfied (Proverbs 27:20). It is a spirit that is never content. There always seems to be a bigger prize up for grabs. Like greed, it is insatiable in its hunger for more accolades, more tokens of power, more titles, and more material things. It brings restlessness over the person who submits to its lure. Once attained, it is always looking for other horizons to conquer. In the end, it can bring isolation and no shared joy in one's never-ending labors (Ecclesiastes 4:8).

Essentially, competition describes when we have a preoccupation with what our eyes see—the lust of the eyes. Also, it conveys an unhealthy focus and competition around what our flesh feels—the lust of the flesh. It also describes our obsession with the accolades and achievements we have accumulated—known as the pride of life. Competition is a spirit of the world rooted in deep insecurity. Hence, the restlessness mentioned earlier.

The spirit of competition is a marked contrast to the Spirit believers have received, the Holy Spirit, who brings security. Believers have the security of knowing the "what" of our blessing as we connect with the Holy Spirit (1 Corinthians 2:12).

Ultimately, we can receive all spiritual gifts available to us as we cry out "Abba Father" (Galatians 4:6).

When we spend quality time with the Holy Spirit, we walk in the pure revelation of the blessings we have freely received. We walk in security, knowing we do not need to fight for it or enter a scarcity spirit of competition.

We understand what Abba Father has already provided for us. We are secure in His provision, like earthly kings or queens tutored to know what they have regarding their rights, privileges, and resources. We also are being guided by the Holy Spirit to understand the inheritance we carry (John 14:26).

Contentment

Godliness with contentment, in contrast to competition, gives us significant gain (1 Timothy 6:6). It gives us peace which anchors our souls in thankfulness. It humbles us to consider how privileged and blessed we are, no matter how chaotic our natural circumstances may be. It is an inner transformation that causes us to always raise our hands in thanksgiving.

Maintaining a continual posture of praise and thanksgiving inoculates us from the disease of competition. It gives us the right viewing point as we survey our lives with eyes of deep gratitude. From there, we realize how easy it can be to forget God's goodness to us.

Remembrance

When our souls and emotions are downcast in roller coaster mode (Lamentations 3:20), we must remind ourselves that we would have no breath without the Creator. Without Him, we would have no gift of sleeping and waking up to a new day. Without our source, we could do nothing (John 15:5). So, we can then understand other hard truths, such as we did not "make" ourselves, and everything we have acquired in life has only been by the grace of God. An understanding that allows us to wear the robes of humility as a steward of the precious grace entrusted to us (1 Peter 4:10).

The truth clings to our mind; we see that it is by His mercy that life's circumstances do not consume us. It is purely by His compassion we have been able to navigate the high seas of tragedy. We bow our knees in recognition of the faithfulness of God to our families and us (Lamentations 3:21–23). Once our mind grasps these timeless truths, our souls and emotions become revived in hope (Lamentations 3:24–26).

There are no little things to thank God for; everything is notable and worthy of thanksgiving (1 Thessalonians 5:18).

In the last days, described as difficult or dangerous, there is a warning that the disease of being unthankful will run rampant in the world as men become lovers of themselves (2 Timothy 3:1–3).

The other warnings are about the dangers of greed, boasting, pride, blasphemy, and disobedience. They also address being unholy, unloving, unforgiving, slanderous, and not demonstrating self-control, describing how we can finally end up in the sorry state described as brutal, despisers of good, traitors, headstrong, haughty, lovers of pleasure rather than lovers of God (2 Timothy 3:4).

These warnings constitute a timely alert, reminding us to carefully observe and examine our behaviors in order to avoid these personal landmines.

Our definition of success must always combine achievement with behavior and character.

Character is the hidden regulator of behavior. A character shaped by continual remembrance, thanksgiving, and contentment will help us avoid any behavior hazards during these uncertain times.

The Greatest Prize

CHAPTER SEVEN NO ONE WINS

It is the goodness of the Lord that has led me to repentance (Romans 2:4). The embrace of His love awakened me to my assignment on the earth and guided me into a transformation miracle (2 Timothy 1:9). My journey of salvation forced me to emerge from the darkness of sin into God's marvelous light (1 Peter 2:9).

I look back on my life, and I see the miracle of growth and maturity as the Lord has led me patiently on the paths of righteousness because I carry His name (Psalm 23:1–3). I have tasted the love of God, and nothing else can ever fully satisfy the thirst in my heart. I live with a constant hunger for His presence and the desire for His Spirit.

All the things I have counted loss to gain Christ have been worth it. I have lost my old life and attained the life intended for me: a life of constant communion with God, which is the most fantastic prize (Philippians 3:8). You will be glad to know that the same shift and prize are equally available to everyone who wants to accept the invitation.

A spiritual invitation to access the constant refreshing water from Christ, so you never need to thirst again (John 4:13).

My Faith Prayer

Lord, help me be content with everything You have blessed me with, as I always respond with a heart of gratitude.

Now godliness with contentment is great gain.
(1 Timothy 6:6, NKJV)

My Relentless Faith Testimonies

Record here the many ways God has amazed you as you relentlessly stretched your faith.

CHAPTER SEVEN   NO ONE WINS

Chapter Eight

Confusion Cloud

Darkness generally brings confusion, but light, by contrast, brings clarity. We should not stumble around in the dark but walk in the light of God's Word (Psalm 119:130). His word gives all the understanding we need.

This chapter is about lifting the veil over different areas of our lives where we may have been walking around in darkness and confusion. In the same way, it says Christ takes off the veil over the Word of God (2 Corinthians 3:14). It is almost like we also need to take off the blindfold we have been wearing to see clearly.

CHAPTER EIGHT   CONFUSION CLOUD

Self

Darkness over who we are can mean we try to open doors not meant for us. Doors can represent breakthroughs. Doors are also essential mechanisms for transition. There is generally warfare attached to every door in life, as I covered in Chapter 2, *My Picture Frame*. By walking through doors not meant for us, we can fight wars also not meant for us.

The first thing we must discover in life is ourselves. Confusion about who we are can rob us of our victory in life.

This discovery journey involves spending time with ourselves and others called by God to journey with us in each season. We must throw light on the darkness of who we are. What is our outlook, and are our motivations? What are our likes and dislikes? What makes us angry?

Before we discover others, we must discover ourselves. We should prioritize spending time with ourselves rather than constantly seeking to be surrounded by other people or busy with too many commitments. In return, we will have the space and time to discover who we are through God's eyes.

As we search through prayer and the Word, we can uncover both the pleasant and not-so-pleasant parts of our lives. We can then evaluate our lives based on God's standard and judge ourselves. Judging ourselves has inestimable spiritual value (1 Corinthians 11:31).

For example, we are encouraged to prayerfully examine ourselves and our relationship with Christ before we engage in Holy Communion (1 Corinthians 11:28).

We are our greatest asset in life, not our jobs, houses, or cars. So we must invest the "gold" of time into really understanding what makes us tick. When we invest this time, we will maximize our life and our impact in life.

Purpose

Darkness over our purpose will also mean we can miss out on opportunities.

Opportunities are divine circumstances meant to transition us through different seasons of life. David experienced the opportunity through Goliath to transition himself from a season of preparation as a shepherd boy to a giant killer in his season of emergence as a warrior in Saul's army (1 Samuel 17).

When we understand our purpose, our eyes can perceive the light of forthcoming opportunities.

The interesting thing about God is that He does not use every opportunity for significant transitions in our lives. The level of significance is also dependent on our current season.

In a season of preparation, what we generally experience can be described as mini or cupcake transitions.

God is a great encourager. Whenever I think of the word encourager now, I think of someone wearing and dressed in courage.

We can have "flashes" and insights into the future during our season of preparation. They bring encouragement to help us stay disciplined and committed to our preparation season. They also remind us not to bail out of it before time. Preparation is a place of serving diligently and faithfully for the future reward.

Thank God David fought the lion and bear while serving his father before fighting Goliath. His lion and bear fight happened in the wilderness of preparation. Nobody else apart from God was aware of these early preparatory hurdles in David's path.

The significant transition Goliath represented only appeared when the opportunity to seal David's transition from his season of preparation to his season of limelight arose.

We must wait for God to announce us after our season of preparation is complete. We must not promote ourselves through premature exposure in our season of preparation. There is a reason why the life chances of a premature baby are less than that of a full-term baby.

We can apply the same analogy to our spiritual growth. Let us not be too eager to step out of our season of preparation until God rings the school bell, stating, "It is time."

Relationships

The greatest asset we have in life other than ourselves is our relationships. Our ability to perceive who

God has surrounded us with will determine whether we receive the maximum blessing appointed to our lives.

Thank God the Shunamite woman perceived Elisha as a prophet. That perception set her to work investing in building an upper room and furnishing it to honor him. His words of ensuing gratitude from her actions held the key to her breakthrough (2 Kings 4:8–17).

When we do not understand the value and importance of relationships, we can easily underrate them. This topic is so important that we will now focus on different types of relationships. This list of relationship types is not exhaustive but purely illustrative to show different dimensions of relationships we need to cultivate.

Destiny Relationships

The destinies of others can connect to our futures. We touched on this also in Chapter 4, *Shadow Fighting*, and the section on fighting destiny when we looked at Moses' destiny connection with the nation of Israel.

We may meet and connect with some people who are signposts in our lives. Sometimes they are signposts of growth, opportunities, favor, danger, tragedy, victory, and defeat. Our response to these people and the signposts they represent are essential cues in our spiritual walk.

Suppose we look at the life of Jesus. Simeon and Anna were signposts of His identity and future (Luke 2:25–38). At twelve, the teachers Jesus met in the temple were signposts of His spiritual growth (Luke 2:42–47). His parents were signposts of His covering for a season, as He went back with them and remained dependent on them until the appointed time (Luke 2:48–51). John the Baptist was a signpost of the favor He carried as the preferred One (John 1:15, 27, 30).

Peter's denial (Luke 22:61) and Judas' betrayal (John 13:18–19) were signposts of the tragedy ahead. The two robbers at the cross were signposts of defeat and victory at the door of death through the power of their choices (Luke 23:39–43). One mocked in his response, the other responded in a cry for mercy. The latter gained his eternal victory of salvation.

CHAPTER EIGHT   CONFUSION CLOUD

Crowd Relationships

God's intention was always for us to live in a community (Psalm 133:1). Jesus was continually surrounded by crowds wherever He went because His value attracted them to various expressions of the anointing over His life.

His fame spread in His early work as a Deliverer (Mark 1:23–28). Then He became famous as a Healer known for healing scores of sick people (Mark 1:32–34). Then He was a Provider, feeding the five thousand (Mark 6:30–44) and the four thousand (Mark 8:1–10). Then He was a Miracle Worker, raising Lazarus from the dead (John 11:38–44). Finally, He became a Savior as he went to the Cross (John 19:17) and Life-Giver as he rose on the third day (John 20:17).

The crowd comes to expose the multiple dimensions of our lives and the anointing we carry, just like Our Lord Jesus Christ. Like Jesus, we need to learn when to embrace the crowd (Mark 8:2) and when to hide (Luke 4:42).

We should not live our lives continually in the public glare. There is a secret place that demands the core part of our lives behind shut doors so that we can appear fleetingly with the crowd to receive our reward in the open (Matthew 6:6).

What we do behind shut doors is what gives us the platforms in the open that God rewards. Many are exhausting what should be many "secret place" hours, standing precariously on manufactured platforms that correspond with men's rewards, not God's.

I learned recently that the anointing for wealth flows from the place of intimacy behind shut doors, as illustrated by the story of The Widow's Oil in 2 Kings 4:4–7.

These are some of the precious benefits of spending time in a secret place when you stumble across these priceless gems of knowledge.

Mentoring Relationships

Thank God for God-given mentors invested in our lives. In the same way our pastors are a gift from God to us, so are mentors. Barnabas was initially a ministry mentor to Paul (Acts 11:24–26).

CHAPTER EIGHT CONFUSION CLOUD

I have had the rare privilege of mentoring many young people on their life journeys, and it has been a gratifying and enriching experience.

However, I once was in a conversation with someone I was mentoring in a particular period. I said to this young lady, "I am not your friend." Essentially, I told her that my best value was being a mentor for her, not a friend. I recognized God had placed me in her life to provide the counsel of a mentor. If she did not realize this, she would lose out on the blessing of mentoring that was available to her.

How we receive people determines what we get out of the relationship. Imagine treating what should be a gold-plated, "fine china" relationship like a common commodity. You will miss the gold; all you will get is the brass you see. We all need to pray an important prayer: "Lord, open my eyes to the value of the relationships around me."

In a season of proximity, the same prophet received in two different ways released different results. The young men who mocked the Prophet Elijah as the bald head received the results of their mocking (2 Kings 2:23–24). The Shunamite woman who recognized the value he carried as a sent man of God secured the long-awaited breakthrough of a child she had desired (2 Kings 4:8–17).

I was initially perplexed when my pastor taught about the danger of familiarity. Later on, I discovered that familiarity could act as a spiritual poison in strategic relationships God places in our lives.

Suppose we become too familiar with people who should be precious pearls in our lives. The pearl qualities they carry become dismissed in the river of familiarity. Once that happens, we can easily cast them down to be trodden by our words and remarks (Matthew 7:6).

I am very deliberate about not getting too close to my leaders. I would rather they be far off, with a healthy distance of separation between us. I would rather err on the side of caution by trembling in Godly reverence at their words than treat them as ordinary furniture on which I can casually rest.

Miriam's story in the Old Testament shows us the danger of familiarity we can encounter even with our family members. We must respect the office each person occupies, even when we recognize some of their shortcomings as none of us is perfect (Number 12:1–16).

Whenever the temptation to speak against someone we should value comes up, the words about not judging another man's servant should shut the door of that downward slide of temptation into familiarity (Romans 14:3–4).

Covenant Relationships

Covenant relationships are the highest order of relationships. They are the highest order because they demand the highest sacrifice in time, commitment, and endurance. They are not casual relationships to be entered into lightly. They are binding relationships that are reference points for our lives.

The word binding indicates relationships based on agreement, carrying an obligation that we should not break. A pastoral relationship is a covenant relationship. God said He would give us shepherds after His own heart (Jeremiah 3:15).

A shepherd protects, covers, provides for, and tends to the needs of the sheep. Essentially, the Good Shepherd, Our Lord, Jesus Christ, laid down His life for His sheep and will expect other shepherds to follow His example (John 10:11,15).

For those who take on this tall order of responsibility for God's sheep, none of these activities are casual. They deserve honor, obedience, and respect (1 Thessalonians 5:12–13).

Pastors are God's choice for us and not our choice, hence the need for careful prayer before joining a church and committing to its pastor.

> *Now we ask you, brothers and sisters, to appreciate those who diligently work among you [recognize, acknowledge, and respect your leaders], who are in charge over you in the Lord and who give instruction.*
> *and [we ask that you appreciate them and] hold them in the highest esteem in love because of their work [on your behalf]. Live in peace with one another.*
>
> 1 Thessalonians 5:12–13 (AMP)

CHAPTER EIGHT CONFUSION CLOUD

The marriage relationship is another covenant relationship that we should not treat lightly. We must exhaust all options to test this relationship before saying, "I do" (1 Timothy 5:24).

Confusion can come when we mix up our relationships. When we treat covenant relationships as crowd relationships, we can experience shipwreck in our Christian walk. It takes the Holy Spirit to help us discern the proper placement of our relationships and their right treatment. Jesus rebuked Jerusalem when they did not recognize their day of visitation; they did not perceive Him and receive Him as their Messiah (Luke 13:34–35). They had unfortunately mismanaged their relationship with Jesus.

With spiritual maturity comes enlightenment and clarity (Ephesians 1:17–18). Maturity equips us with the right level of wisdom to operate in discernment in our relationships. Jesus increased in wisdom, stature, and favor with God and men (Luke 2:52). If Jesus needed both favor with God and with men, we would also need the same to reign in life as He did (Romans 5:17).

So far, we have considered the different areas where confusion could creep into our lives. Let us now observe the effects of confusion.

Effects of Confusion

Confusion generally comes from a firm root of fear which brings indecision. There is wavering between two opinions spoken about in the Bible (1 Kings 18:21).

The Word of God is always a definitive Yes and Amen (2 Corinthians 1:20). Suppose we look at the character of Jesus. He was always definite in His actions after His time of prayer and seeking the will of the Father.

Once He knew the Father's will, He moved with boldness and courage (Luke 6:12–13). There was no hesitation from Him when challenged in spiritual battles. He had a strong sense of who He was and the authority He carried (Mark 9:25–26). He remained unflustered in any situation (Mark 9:27).

We also have the mind of Christ, which brings clarity to issues (1 Corinthians 2:16). We must always surround ourselves with the promises of God in His Word and the

CHAPTER EIGHT   CONFUSION CLOUD

prophecies spoken over us. We must never lose sight of them as they kick-start faith in our hearts, bringing soundness and balance in our minds and the power to move forward (Romans 10:17). The backdrop of countless relatable testimonies in the Bible also gives us a strong bedrock of confidence to move forward.

Confusion can bring a spiritual cloud that brings a measure of haziness over our minds if left unattended. Sometimes it robs us of perspective. Other times, we can lose the nuances amid confusion. Confusion can be like wading in the deep mud of indecision. We can quickly become weighed down by doubts, questions, and a heavy sense of inertia.

Sometimes confusion can come in bouts, gripping our hearts as we wrestle with it. I recently had to make a significant decision to leave the familiar behind. I chose to step out of a particular boat after many years of paddling in shallow waters.

What initially seemed exciting and liberating became more demanding when the moment came to step onto the water of the unknown at God's instruction.

The usual safety nets and comfort rails were gone, and the reality of the wind of change faced me head-on.

As a human race, we are predominantly creatures of routine and comfort. Stepping into the unfamiliar can often release a torrential factory of butterflies within our emotions. However, I have learned that obedience is better than sacrifice. In my experience, I have found that despite any discomfort through many seasons of difficulty. To follow God's instructions is always better than any counterfeit action, which may provide temporary comfort.

Every time we stretch our faith, we create a greater capacity to believe God for more.

Remember the first time you laid down a large seed in your giving and how much it stretched you. In hindsight, that first seed was just a landing mat for the more significant sacrifices that awaited if you chose to swing higher on the parallel bars of life.

The more you stretch your faith muscle, the stronger it becomes. So you can carry the greater weight of God's promises.

CHAPTER EIGHT   CONFUSION CLOUD

I pray our lives will always be great faith wombs God can use to incubate His miraculous plan of destiny.

My Faith Prayer

Lord, let the light of dawn break into every cloud of confusion hovering over my life.

The people who sat in darkness
have seen a great light,
And upon those who sat in
the region and shadow of death
Light has dawned."
(Matthew 4:16, NKJV)

CHAPTER EIGHT   CONFUSION CLOUD

My Relentless Faith Testimonies

Record here the many ways God has amazed you as you relentlessly stretched your faith.

Chapter Nine

Distractions, Distractions, Distractions

Have you ever observed someone who is distracted? I have experienced this to varying degrees, and I still face this challenge daily. The critical characteristic I have noticed is the quick loss of concentration.

Reading a book can be likened to eating a piece of fruit. Much of the initial sweet juice flows effortlessly in the early chapters, with great enjoyment. As we progress, we must now tackle the chunkier and more challenging pieces of the fruit. Though much tougher, this is also where the best nutrients are.

By the same analogy, if we can persevere through the penultimate chapters of a book without getting distracted, it holds the promise of the best nutrients like the piece of fruit and will do us a tremendous amount of good.

Distractions are an unavoidable aspect of life that affect us all. So, let's dive in as we prepare to digest all of this chapter's solid fruit on how to manage distractions.

Concentration

I used to take great pride in having days bursting at the seams with activities. I enjoyed being a whirlwind of activity, ticking many things off on my to-do list. However, despite all the whirl of energy, I would not have much tangible evidence of fully completed goals at the end of the year. After many years of failure in this area, I learned that there is great power in concentration.

Concentration gives you the fullness of the power of focus. Concentration changes and shifts things that could never move casually. With greater attention comes a greater force for movement and progress. In my case, I have achieved more in one month by concentrating on

CHAPTER NINE DISTRACTIONS, DISTRACTIONS, DISTRACTIONS

fewer priority activities around my goals than the last year of buzzing around with disjointed activities as a busy bee!

I have discovered that the world indeed belongs to those who are concentrated. Every time we lose concentration, we lose an advantage.

Like many others reading this book, interruptions were the big trigger for my lack of focus. So, I had to knuckle down and look at my schedule. I decided to devote my most concentrated effort to my highest priority matters for the day.

I am a morning person, so if I could hit my stride very early in the morning before the rest of the world woke up, I would be on to a winner.

This winning start would allow me to spend my first five working hours tackling those priorities. After that, the rest of the day would become more manageable, including the reward of an earlier finish. However, to hit the bullseye of my early morning stride, I had to win the battle the night before and get to bed early!

We tend to lose at least three advantages when we become distracted and lose concentration. These three advantages are time, focus, and leverage. We will examine each of these areas as we look at the following sections of this book on how to counteract these losses.

Determination

Determination is a crucial trait that allows us to maintain our time advantage. The world belongs to those who are determined as well as concentrated.

Most things in life do not align with a linear equation for the mathematicians or a monotonous sequence of sentences for the linguists. That would be too predictable. Instead, we typically experience a jagged pattern of ups and downs. There are always surprises and curveballs in life.

Curveballs, however, do not move the determined. The determined use those unexpected events to anchor them in an unwavering focus on their goal. Like failure heroes who have learned to harness failures to their advantage, which we covered in Chapter Six, determina-

CHAPTER NINE DISTRACTIONS, DISTRACTIONS, DISTRACTIONS

tion also allows us to embrace any curve balls that come our way as a sign to press down even harder on our goal.

Suppose we start on a task and do not hunker down in determination when those curveballs come up. We may then have to restart that cycle again. When that happens, we can lose our time investment and advantage.

That curveball may be the fear of going into your promised land, which Israel experienced as they circled various mountains in the wilderness (Deuteronomy 1:6, Deuteronomy 2:1–3). They lost the time advantage of forty years because they allowed fear and unbelief to rob them of their determination. If their resolve had remained intact, the children of Israel could eventually have broken through with their faith in God's Word.

The *Book of Hebrews* tells us that faith alone is not enough. We also need endurance or rugged determination to obtain promises by remaining anchored in obedience through our faith (Hebrews 10:36).

Successful entrepreneurs, especially serial entrepreneurs, have mastered the discipline of determination through many adverse circumstances. When you listen to their stories, they are generally full of many instances in which they could easily have thrown in the towel.

But instead of quitting, they pushed against the status quo to survive and flourish. They became determined not to give up despite the bleak circumstances. They often realized they had invested too much effort and time to back down now. Giving up was not an option, a no-go area in their minds. They were willing to work harder, be more creative, and keep determinedly pushing until they found a way of "escape" to make it work.

Success usually shows up on our doorstep through opportunities created through hard work and determination.

Planes, like entrepreneurs, usually take off with a target destination in mind. However, somewhere along the journey, they typically experience turbulence. The determined pilot knows these circumstances are just a prompt to take the plane higher.

I have learned similar lessons in my entrepreneurial journey. I also started with a destination in mind for

CHAPTER NINE DISTRACTIONS, DISTRACTIONS, DISTRACTIONS

the business. But then I hit the turbulence of a nervy pandemic landscape. I knew it was time to take my vision higher by evolving the business model, approach, and target customers. For a determined entrepreneur, survival has a peculiar way of creating innovation, especially if giving up is not an option.

For the believer walking in covenant with Christ, this is where the Lord hears our voice and opens our eyes like Hagar to see the well of water we need to survive (Genesis 21:19).

When we are between a rock and a hard place, we become candidates for God to demonstrate His miraculous power as He did with Moses by parting the Red Sea (Exodus 14:16).

How will you ever experience the God of miracles if you have never been in a tight spot where all other options apart from a miracle have been discarded? Especially when the fear is palpable amongst those you are leading.

Like Moses, the sight of Pharaoh's thunderous marching army approaching ever closer had already created fear in the hearts of the people he was leading (Exodus 14:10–12).

Moses knew he must urgently address this fear (Exodus 14:13–14). Moses's experience showed the reality of the Christian leadership paradox. Addressing fear in the heart of followers, God has called you to lead with faith-filled words when you may also be fearful.

However, regardless of fear, you must then have the confidence to go to your secret place, cry out to God, and receive His instruction for His people in the same way Moses did (Exodus 14:15–18).

Now armed with the courage of God's instructions, you can lead fear-filled followers into the next miraculous place that God has instructed.

Consistency

Distractions also rob us of consistency. Without consistency, we can lose the focus advantage. I have lost the focus advantage on completing essential projects too many times to count. It was effortless for me to be consistent at the start; I loved starting new things. But

CHAPTER NINE DISTRACTIONS, DISTRACTIONS, DISTRACTIONS

to dig in for the middle and to completion was where my struggle lay.

Consistency is the amplifier of our efforts. We continually improve ourselves through consistency.

In the spiritual context, those who understand the importance of consistency in their daily quiet time with God will appreciate its power. They apply consistency to their Bible study, prayer, fasting, and other spiritual disciplines. After a few years, you see them flourishing with exceptional spiritual knowledge and authority. The tiny seed sown can now provide the shade of covering for others in its grown tree state (Mark 4:30–32).

Consistency helps our roots to go down deep in God, so we are not swayed continually by every wind of deceitful doctrine (Ephesians 4:14).

We can never experience growth fully if we do not put our roots down somewhere and give ourselves the space and time to grow. No plant can ever achieve its full potential if uprooted continually.

Small Improvements

Small improvements help to ensure we keep our leverage advantage. This section will help us unpack that statement.

Firstly, we need to understand that skill comes by constant adjustments or fine-tuning of a gift. The skill comes as the talent goes through the connection of many minor improvements along the way.

A mindset of small improvements constantly reviews its results and asks what needs to be tweaked further for a better outcome.

If we can ask and answer the previous question after every new experience. Then, we are progressing rapidly towards establishing an outstanding growth and development mindset.

What is needed could be just a tiny adjustment in approach. Maybe you need a fresh "new wineskin" perspective. Perhaps you need to break out of hardened thinking patterns that have always led to the same result.

CHAPTER NINE DISTRACTIONS, DISTRACTIONS, DISTRACTIONS

You may need to expose yourself to others who break the mold and rut you are stuck in by their challenge to be a better version of yourself.

Without minor improvements, we can lose the leverage advantage. To understand the leverage advantage even better, let us look at the concept of a lever.

Levers generally help us to lift greater loads with less effort. Note those words: *with less effort*. We often think the answer is to work harder, but that may not be the case. Using the pruning lever to bear more fruit (John 15) may not require more effort. It may just involve pruning our mindset, approach, and positioning. For a believer, this is where the Holy Spirit partners with them, giving them the leverage advantage of His mighty power.

Recently I have been praying a lot about positioning. I reflected on some of the past books I have written. I conversed with the Holy Spirit about their positioning.

A common saying that proves instructive when discussing positioning is, "Don't throw the baby out with the bath water." A lot of times, the issue may not be with the baby. You can throw away the bathwater without throwing away the baby. The content may not be the challenge. The challenge may be the content positioning in the wrong bathwater.

That last sentence may be the lightbulb moment someone reading this book has, which could change their lives forever.

Many innovations we celebrate today had their origins focused on solving another problem. The inventor likely evaluated their creation with the mindset of small improvements. Such evaluation often results in a shift to its application. With this shift suddenly to the inventor's utter astonishment, their creation experiences an unexpected explosion in the marketplace. From then on, the rest is history, as the common saying goes.

There was a willingness from the inventor to change, tweak something, and shine a light in some undiscovered sweet spot to experience the complete fulfillment of the idea's potential.

I have a friend who taught me this principle inadvertently. I noticed how she maximized her "one talent." She did not focus on quantity but quality. Like the wid-

CHAPTER NINE DISTRACTIONS, DISTRACTIONS, DISTRACTIONS

ow who pulled on the Prophet Elisha's grace in 1 Kings 4, she poured her one gift out into many vessels.

I say this to deliver many multi-talented individuals who never fully maximize each gift's potential. They often do not give each talent the benefit of focus and making minor improvements to harness it to its full potential.

Now, we have covered the three advantages of time, focus, and leverage, that distractions around concentration can cost us, and how to remedy them through determination, consistency, and small improvements. We will move on to the awareness of other types of distractions.

Facing the Future

Distractions of the past can keep our lives anchored in the past. These historical distractions may not just be failures. Equally, previous successes can also become distractions that stop us from running toward the future.

The moving future train has pulled into its planned stop waiting for the ready. It is prepared for those willing to trade in the sentimentality of the past and jump on the unfamiliar carriages of the future.

A lie we may have entertained is that we need to wait until we are entirely free of past burdens before jumping on the train of the future.

Are you willing to remain on the platform of yesterday when the moving train of tomorrow is within your grasp?

I recently had a dream that summarises this section of the book well. In the first scene of the dream, I was sitting on what looked like a subway. I was watching someone speaking about past successes. Others surrounded them, reliving all the details of their past accomplishments.

Fast forward to the next scene in the dream. I saw myself on a platform next to a train that had just pulled into its stop. I was standing first with someone I knew who was younger than me, and then later I saw someone older than me, who I also knew. With each person, I was saying my goodbyes. I remember doing so hurriedly while I ran to catch the train. I was carrying a backpack

CHAPTER NINE DISTRACTIONS, DISTRACTIONS, DISTRACTIONS

and just about made it onto the already moving train as the doors were about to close. When I got on the train, I was met by a carriage of unfamiliar faces.

This dream led me to a personal conclusion that the future is not about our age but our desire. Like the parable Jesus gave, I desired the new wine, so I was willing to sacrifice the familiarity of the old to embrace the new (Luke 5:37–39). It also showed me that I had no interest in joining those celebrating the applause of past achievements when there was much more ahead of me.

My Faith Prayer

Lord, help me to maintain my focus on You by not getting distracted by the noise of life.

You will keep him in perfect peace,
Whose mind is stayed on You,
Because he trusts in You.
(Isaiah 26:3, NKJV)

CHAPTER NINE DISTRACTIONS, DISTRACTIONS, DISTRACTIONS

My Relentless Faith Testimonies

Record here the many ways God has amazed you as you relentlessly stretched your faith.

Chapter Ten

Restoration Fire

Faith is a restorer of lost things. How can I say that so confidently? Faith restores because faith calls those things that do not exist as though they did (Romans 4:17). Notice that faith calls.

How does faith call? Faith calls through pronouncements and declarations of God's words which always activate the fire of restoration.

We must recognize that The Bible is not an ordinary book. Far from it, The Bible is an extraordinary book of fiery, supernatural, power-packed, and life-restoring words because it came from the inspiration of God.

God and His Word are the same—relentless in their enduring power of restoration, which remains unshaken for eternity. His words last forever (Matthew 24:35).

So let's get ready to see the miraculous as we make the bold faith calls in this final chapter in alignment with God's Covenant Word.

Covenant faith calls us from every lowly and hidden place into the place prepared for us as sons and daughters of the King of kings (Romans 9:25–26). Faith tells us that we are ready for our royal robes, signet ring, and the embrace and celebration of the Father. The end of the waiting season for lost sons and daughters returning home in restoration (Luke 15:11–27).

Our restoration story is not just about salvation and our identity but also about restoring everything else we have lost through the hard knocks of life.

As the prophecy in the Book of Joel announces, God will restore our time and honor. It also says God will restore our spiritual heritage supernaturally through prophecies, dreams, and visions. Our restoration then promises to revive nations to the ends of the earth (Joel 2:18–32).

In the years after the global reset of 2020, many have experienced so much loss in many areas of life. How can we expect restoration?

We need to realize that some things always go together in the restoration calendar, with one preceding the other. The darkness of the night always comes before the breaking light of day. Similarly, there is usually a prolonged drought before the pouring rain. Famine has to be followed by harvest, brokenness by healing, and the ravages of war generally shift into the fire of revival. Finally, loss always precedes restoration.

Calling for Continual Bread

It seems only fitting that as we conclude this book, to come back to the story of the restoration of Mephibosheth, which we started at the outset of this book in Chapter 1 and Chapter 2. In the first two chapters, we saw the first type of restoration that Mephibosheth experienced regarding the provision for him.

We learned he moved from being forsaken into a season of eating continual bread at David's table, with land restored to him and servants to cultivate the land. We have already covered these elements in detail in earlier chapters. So the rest of this chapter will focus primarily on other aspects of Mephibosheth's story of restoration. We will also look at different dimensions of the powerful call to restoration in the lives of Elisha and Peter.

Calling for Honor

The second aspect of Mephibosheth's restoration story is a calling back to his honor as a king's son. From the low place in Lo Debar, he received the call into the palace to sit at the kings' table (2 Samuel 9:5–7). Ziba, who previously was walking in what should have been Mephibosheth's princely heritage, was now realigned back to his place as one of Mephibosheth's servants (2 Samuel 9:9–12).

A useful scripture in the *Book of Ecclesiastes* highlights the travesty of servants riding horses. While at the same time, princes walk (Ecclesiastes 10:7), which had been

CHAPTER TEN   RESTORATION FIRE

Mephibosheth's story previously until his restoration call from King David.

In the same way, Mephibosheth's seat of honor was calling for him. Many of God's covenant sons and daughters have walked out of their princely heritage and are now receiving the call back to their seats from every low place they have been living (Luke 15:11–32).

God's princes and princesses hear the call out of the beggarly place they have been languishing through incidents of brokenness in life. Wherever they have felt lame, they receive the covenant call back to sonship and their rightful place at the king's table (2 Samuel 9:7,11).

Sin and its unintended consequences shall no longer have dominion over God's precious sons and daughters (Romans 6:14). There will be no more entanglement of bondage over God's anointed ones (Galatians 5:1).

We release them into their destined place in God (Ephesians 2:6). They carry the emblem of the royal seal of the blood of Jesus over their lives (Revelation 1:5). So, we call them back into righteousness (2 Corinthians 6:17–18). We call them back into their place of maturity (Philippians 3:14–15).

Calling for Joy

Thirdly for Mephibhoseth, it was a story of calling out from the darkness, hiddenness, shame, and lameness into the joy of acceptance through his father's covenant with David (2 Samuel 9:7).

Many of God's sons and daughters have wandered in darkness, despair, and shame for too long, and we call them back into the light (Matthew 4:16). We call them back into the fullness of joy. We call them back from desperate circumstances that robbed them of their dignity. We call them back into fellowship beyond broken hearts and shattered expectations (Luke 4:18). We call them back into the promises of their Father (Acts 2:39).

We call them back as fathers and mothers to nations and patriarchs in God's kingdom. We declare their joy will be complete again as they walk in the fullness of their assignment (Psalm 16:11).

We call many sons and daughters back from confusion (Isaiah 61:7); we call them back from danger. We call them back from the sorrow over many lost opportunities (Jeremiah 31:12). We call them back to be repair-

CHAPTER TEN   RESTORATION FIRE

ers of bridges and the brokenness in the world as they minister to others (Isaiah 58:12).

> *And they shall rebuild the old ruins,*
> *They shall raise up the former desolations,*
> *And they shall repair the ruined cities,*
> *The desolations of many generations.*
> *Strangers shall stand and feed your flocks,*
> *And the sons of the foreigner*
> *Shall be your plowmen and your vinedressers.*
> *But you shall be named the priests of the LORD,*
> *They shall call you the servants of our God.*
> *You shall eat the riches of the Gentiles,*
> *And in their glory you shall boast.*
> *Instead of your shame you shall have double honor,*
> *And instead of confusion they shall rejoice in their portion.*
> *Therefore in their land they shall possess double;*
> *Everlasting joy shall be theirs.*
> (Isaiah 61:4–7, NKJV)

Calling for the Prophet

In addition to Mephibosheth, we also see the story of restoration emerge with the prophet Elisha. Elisha was an unusual prophet. He picked up the prophetic baton from Elijah, the fireworks prophet. His predecessor, Elijah's ministry hallmark, was releasing the judgment of God.

Elisha, however, carried a different type of prophetic anointing. He had a restoration anointing, as seen in the miracles he performed. Each one, if we think about it, was about restoration.

The wealth of the widow with the oil restored (2 Kings 4:1–7). The commander, Naaman's flesh, became restored from leprosy as he dipped in the Jordan seven times (2 Kings 5:1–14). The heritage of the Shunamite woman received restoration through her miracle child (2 Kings 4:8–17). Even when that child was about to be snatched by death later in life, Elisha was on hand to perform a restoration miracle by raising the dead child back to life (2 Kings 4:18–37).

Elisha demonstrated the prophetic dimension of restoration. In all the miracles he performed, the restoration came through declarations or acts of faith as each person followed the prophet's instructions. Elisha's life clearly shows the power of prophetic words and instructions.

We see this also typified in Jesus' ministry. He encouraged others to activate their faith through their declarations: what do you want me to do for you? He asked blind Bartimaeus (Mark 10:51). It was an invitation to the blind man to declare his miracle.

Actions also proved crucial in other cases in Jesus' ministry. People like the man at the pool of Bethesda, who had lost hope after thirty-eight years of infirmity, now asked to take up his bed to walk (John 5:8).

In each case, as each one stretched the capacity of their faith, spectacular miracles emerged to the glory of God. Indeed, no one can do these signs unless God was with Him, echoed the Jewish teacher Nicodemus, a solid endorsement of Jesus as the Teacher Who came from the Father (John 3:1–2).

We continue with Elisha's story.

Elisha dealt with the root of issues as he located the source of bitter waters and poured salt prophetically into it. He then declared healing over the waters (2 Kings 2:19–22).

We are told in 2 Chronicles 20:20 that establishment comes through believing God's Word, and prosperity comes through the release of faith as we believe in His prophets. Prophets are representatives of God, and as we believe in them, we acknowledge that they are agents of God. Jesus also gave this example in John 17:21.

In a time of famine, a whole nation was kept alive through the prophetic word of Elisha (2 Kings 7:1). This provides insight into the power of the prophetic word.

Calling for Victory

Finally, Mephibosheth received the call from a place of loss into victory.

The best way to imagine victory is in contrast to loss. The best way we can imagine the mountain is in comparison to the valley. The best way the harvest can be pictured is in contrast to the famine. The seven fat cows contrast with the seven gaunt cows (Genesis 41:18–21). The seven full heads contrast with the seven thin heads (Genesis 41:22–23). Extremes on opposite ends of the spectrum help our imagination to appreciate the magnitude of the restoration power involved.

Mephibosheth moved from the house of Machir in Lo Debar to the home of King David. Where you are will determine your experience, whether in helplessness or victory. Mephibosheth's story illustrates this perfectly as he moved from a place of defeat in Lo Debar to success at King David's table.

Your circumstance can easily change on the day of your announcement, as we also see in Joseph's story (Genesis 41:14). One day, he was a prisoner. After his announcement, he was second only to Pharaoh regarding the throne. The transitions happened suddenly for both Mephibhoseth and Joseph after their announcements. Once announced, they were both sent for immediately (2 Samuel 9:3–5, Genesis 41:12–14).

An announcement is here for many lives who suddenly need to shift into victory. It does not matter how long you have been in prison or Lo Debar. Once you receive the announcement of your name, that settles it.

The many forgotten should prepare for remembrance. The many overlooked should prepare for recognition. Those who have had no help, prepare for your recommendation. Those short-changed will need to prepare for reward.

We rejoice to see the great salvation God has prepared for His people in this season of restoration. In this new season, the torn clothes of the past are being made brand new. Damaged reputations are mended. Stormy and severely fractured relationships are becoming healed. Crushed hearts restored. The fragments of lives scattered by bad storms are coming back together, even stronger than before.

In this season, many will receive their decorative garments with clean linen and robes of glory (Revelation 19:8). Their crowns of victory prepared with the burnishing and polishing of shiny medals (Psalm 8:5–6).

It is your season of restoration. The storm is over, and now there is peace. There is calm now after the wind. After the flood, rest.

CHAPTER TEN   RESTORATION FIRE

My prayer is for the Lord to clothe you with peace and give you rest in this season. I see the colors of spring blooming and emerging in your life after the most profound winter season. The heaviness has now shifted to expectancy.

We clap you into rejoicing and celebration. We decree this is your season of turnaround. We proclaim your last season can no longer hold you bound, and we release you into your next season.

We raise the trumpet. We extend the clarion call. We extend the cymbals. We lift the volume of the new song written as the soundtrack for your new season. We strike the high notes; we prepare the drumroll. We tap the keys. We make a joyful noise for the Lord's great deliverance.

I love the before and after picture of restoration. It reveals the depth of love God holds for His children and how intricately He orchestrates His masterpiece of restoration. It is a timeless classic, a bestseller, a praise in the earth.

Many overcomers will celebrate as their faith has the last word over defeat. Many will testify of the exploits of their faith with incredible testimonies, serving as a word of encouragement and triumph to others.

Calling for Revival

The Global reset of the pandemic awakened us to the reality that many people are desperately holding on to things with no eternal promise in an age where lawlessness abounds. It presents a pivotal opportunity for Christians to sound the revival trumpets of the message of the Lord Jesus Christ.

In an age where selfishness abounds, there is a need to proclaim the revival news of the eternal sacrifice on the Cross. In an age where criticism and condemnation abound, it will be a welcome relief to hear the revival message of the acceptance of agape love. In an age where mental health meltdown abounds, we must sound the revival benefits of a sound mind. When nations are raging and factions are rising, many need to hear about the revival approach of eternal peace.

We have a gospel of unconditional love which has delivered generations in the past. It will continue to do so for this current generation and many future generations.

We have a gospel of hope that lifted prior generations. This gospel will also raise a current generation and many future generations when they hear the timeless message about the love of Christ and His eternal sacrifice for them through His death, burial, and resurrection by the power of the Holy Spirit.

> "Rain down, you heavens, from above,
> And let the skies pour down righteousness;
> Let the earth open, let them bring forth salvation,
> And let righteousness spring up together.
> I, the LORD, have created it.
>
> (Isaiah 45:8, NKJV)

Calling Us Out of the Boat

Whenever I read about Peter in his early years of ministry with Jesus, the thought generally whirring in my mind is: who does that?

Like the rest of us in our early years, Peter started his faith journey as a "who does that" type of person. Who tells Jesus that He will not go to the Cross? Who interrupts a significant spiritual moment of Transfiguration to talk about building tents? Who boasts that they will never deny Jesus? Who jumps into the sea very close to the shore, deciding to swim rather than stay in the boat? That was Peter's reaction once he recognized the Master.

Who is Peter? Peter reminds me of myself in my early years of walking in faith. Often I boldly spoke before I realized what I was saying. I had an overestimation of my abilities. I bragged about what Jesus was doing with me. I acted hastily. I spoke more than I listened.

Hopefully, many will recognize themselves in the mirror of Peter's life. Despite Peter's shortcomings, there must have been some merit in him for Jesus to

CHAPTER TEN   RESTORATION FIRE

choose him as the trusted disciple to lead the church after His death and resurrection.

Peter had natural leadership qualities. He was always at the forefront of all that was going on. However, he became a different leader when he collided with taking responsibility for the early church.

We see another Peter emerging in the *Book of Acts*—another type of leader pivoting a church with boldness after a spiritual revival. A revival that would push the frontiers of the church beyond Jerusalem, Judea, and Samaria to the ends of the earth.

Peter's transformation as the leader now at the forefront of the church started after his final "fishing" encounter with Jesus Christ in John 21. This encounter concluded the restoration in Peter's life after the heartbreak of his denial and abandonment of Jesus in His hour of greatest need. Towards the end of the encounter, the Lord effectively reminded Peter that his actions needed to speak louder than his words from that point forward (John 21:15–19).

However, one thing about Peter that stood out was his application of everything he heard from Jesus. From the launching out of his net at the Master's word (Luke 5) to the profound revelation of who Jesus was (Matthew 18). He was not a theoretician who wanted to consent only his mind to Jesus by appreciating His teaching mentally. He was a practitioner—an action-oriented man who wanted to see the results of these words displayed clearly in his life.

Not unexpected from a hardened fisherman used to the practical demonstration of results.

When Peter saw the Lord Jesus walking on water, the only instruction he desired was for Jesus to call for him also to walk on water. "Command me to come," he shouted. True intimacy and belief for him came through experience (Matthew 14:22–33, NKJV).

I have shared many laughs about how Peter doubted and almost failed. However, those willing to look through the eyes of faith may see things differently.

They may appreciate Peter's tremendous courage in taking the risk to step out of the boat and exercise his faith. They may conclude that Peter at least tried to use his faith. Unlike the other disciples, who remained comfortable in the relative safety of the boat, Peter seemed willing to step out of his comfort zone at the opportunity presented to him.

Who commanded Peter to come? The King who had the word of life. The Savior who raised the dead to life and gave sight to the blind, healed every disease, commanded demons, multiplied seed, and had the Spirit without measure. The only One given the power of eternal judgment.

So this was no ordinary beckoning to Peter. He trusted Jesus enough to step out of the boat and walk on water.

Jesus never rebuked Peter for stepping out of the boat. The only rebuke he received was doubting when he saw the wind. However, as soon as Peter cried out, Jesus caught him and stopped him from drowning.

Peter was the only disciple who experienced the miracle of walking on water. It became his testimony of faith—a testimony of a living and active faith, not a theory.

What parallels can we draw from Peter's story? No matter how comfortable we may be, we will never experience the miracle of walking on water by remaining in the safety of the boat in life.

Faith always involves a stretch beyond our comfort zone as we step out of the boat at Jesus's command.

Despite the wind, if we keep our eyes focused on Jesus, we will always experience the miracle of triumph through our faith.

Jesus will never rebuke us for stepping out of the boat by faith at His command. Like Peter, the Lord will help us every step of the way as we commit to walking by faith, even if we get into doubt along the way.

As we continue and faith overcomes doubt, we, too, will experience the supernatural miracle of walking on water with Jesus. A phenomenal testimony of relentlessly exercising our faith in these unsettling times. Glory! Hallelujah!

CHAPTER TEN   RESTORATION FIRE

My Faith Prayer

Lord, help me to become a faith firebrand for You. I don't want to live a life without taking faith risks.

When Jesus heard it, He marveled, and said to those who followed, "Assuredly, I say to you, I have not found such great faith, not even in Israel! (Matthew 8:10, NKJV)

My Relentless Faith Testimonies

Record here the many ways God has amazed you as you relentlessly stretched your faith.

CHAPTER TEN   RESTORATION FIRE

The Prayer of Salvation

I talk so much in this book about a call to live a life of unwavering and relentless faith. However, an even more fundamental call for your life comes before that call.

I want you to have the opportunity of a lifetime to commit your life to the One and only true Savior if you have not already done so.

I should know. I spent the first thirty years of my life running from Him and running towards the arms of things that could never satisfy me.

What do you feel you will need to give up to take up this call? Is it clubbing, drinking, or living an "easy" life with no boundaries? A life with no accountability, full of selfish and prideful intentions only.

I have been there and bought the T-shirt. I still remember my mum's plaintive cry to try going to church on Sundays.

Consider this—what does it profit you to gain all these fleeting things? While in the process, you lose the never-ending opportunity to have a close, intimate walk with the One who created you for a specific purpose.

Holy Spirit, my dearest prayer is that you speak to each person reading this book and show them that the only life worth living is one filled with the love of the Father who gave His best for them.

If you are convinced, then please say this prayer with me.

> *Lord Jesus, I confess I am a sinner who has done my own thing up to this point in my life. I have rebelled against You and Your Word. I am deeply sorry for that. I now understand that You indeed paid the ul-*

timate price for me by shedding Your blood to take away all my sin and shame.

I accept Your gift of salvation, and I declare that You are my Lord and Savior from this point onwards. Amen.

Congratulations, the angels in heaven are doing proverbial backflips, rejoicing at your coming into the household of believers.

Your next step is to find a Bible-believing church where you can hear the Word of God, fellowship with other believers, and grow in faith.

WELCOME INTO GOD'S FAMILY.

Funmbi Ariyo
London, United Kingdom
anointedforleadership1@gmail.com

Milton Keynes UK
Ingram Content Group UK Ltd.
UKHW020742110724
445512UK00011B/281